COMBAT MEDIC:

A soldier's story of the Iraq war and PTSD

By: S. M. Boney IV

Cover by Angry Chair Designs

Edited by Julie Boney Special thanks to H.J Harry

TO ALEAH AND JESSICA:

Thank you for being the shining stars that keep guiding me through the darkness in my life. I'm blessed to be loved by you.

Warning: the language and actions that take place in this book may come across as offensive to some. It is not my intention to offend anyone; I've written everything from memory to help you understand what it's like to be a combat medic in the Army at war. Nothing about it is pretty.

Prelude

Slamming the door, I locked it and rested my head against the wood frame, trying to regain my thoughts. *You're home…you're safe.*

Sunlight is beaming in through the blinds, making it hard to see. Leaning against the marble counter in the kitchen, I set my keys down before wiping the sweat that wasn't there from my brow. I wondered, *Does it ever stop?* My angst was making me feel cold. *No…it never will.* I stared at the floor. *What if I was dead? Would anybody really care? I wouldn't have to deal with this pain anymore. The thoughts; the nightmares…*

My lower back throbbed. I pushed myself up on my hands, thrusting my hips back and forth, waiting for the pain to go away. I closed my eyes, put my head down, and started taking deep breaths, trying to calm down.

Standing up I grabbed a glass of water when a loud bang shook the room. My heart started racing; a chill ran through my body. The hearing in my right ear fell out, leaving a high-pitched ringing in the background. My heart jumped then started beating faster. I closed my eyes and saw flashing lights and heard gunfire – echoes and bangs.

I squatted to the ground behind the counter with my eyes wide open staring at the door. A chill ran through my back, into my heart. My jaw started shaking; teeth chattering like I was stark naked in a blizzard.

Someone kicked down the door dressed in battered, torn clothes with dirty rags covering his face. He ran towards me with an AK-47 rifle pointed at my face, shouting gibberish. I felt a rifle in my hand, the weight of the barrel upon my fingers; but it wasn't there. I felt naked without a weapon, cold and unsafe.

My heart felt like it was being pulled in four different directions. It thumped, pumping me full of cold blood and adrenaline. My mind raced. *What should I do?* I smelled gunfire and smoke, but I could see that I was in my apartment. *Is this real?* The back of my throat was sore; there was a bad, acidic taste in my mouth.

I took in a couple of shallow breaths then jumped up and ran over to the kitchen. I grabbed the handle of my 8-inch chef knife and pulled it from the drawer figuring it would be better to have a weapon in case it wasn't my imagination. I turned toward the door crouched down, waiting for anything that came through.

A minute slowly passed. "This isn't real." I thought out loud, "What am I doing? This is crazy." At that moment excruciating pain shot from my mid-back down to my left foot. It was like someone had sliced my back in half with a searing hot knife. I tried taking a deep breath in, but stopped short when pain wrapped around my lung.

I dropped the knife. Feeling dizzy and nauseated, I slowly walked over to the bathroom, flipped the light on, and stood over the toilet, holding my stomach and head. I was sweating hard now. The room started spinning as an overwhelming smell of gunpowder filled it.

Images from war started shooting through my mind. In one, I was holding pressure on a wound, trying to stop the bleeding from a severed leg. In another, blood was splattered all over a sand-covered ground. Specialist B pointed to the blood, then over to a building. I raised my weapon as we went in for the kill. The last image was of eyes. A pair of glazed over, hauntingly sky blue eyes. They were staring directly into mine. I stared blankly into the toilet, engulfed in those eyes. The sight of death captivated me. I wanted it; it wanted me. It almost had me.

My focus shifted from his eyes to his head. I started to see blood running down his face as it came into focus. A green aid bandage was wrapped around it, attempting to hold his severed skull together. I looked down and saw blood covering my hands. I knew it wasn't really there, but it all felt so real.

At that moment I felt numb, emptiness grew inside; my chest slowly became cold. Icy blood pumped through my veins. It felt like I was dying; like life was being drained out of me. I started shaking as a chill crept through me. Death enveloped me, clutching my soul with a wanton lust. My spirit quaked as my heart blackened.

Tears started falling down my cheeks as the visions slowly faded away. I felt like a hollow shell, void of any substance of life. Shaking my head I wiped the tears, but kept crying; unable to stop myself.

I walked to my bedroom, empty except for a small dresser. It's been 7 months since I moved and still no furniture. Saddened, I closed the door and opened the window. A cool breeze blew through. The sun was bright, warm, and comforting. I took in a couple deep breaths; my jaw still jittered from the flashback as I let it out. My shirt was drenched in sweat.

I opened the drawer of the dresser and grabbed my pipe and weed. I ground some up, put it in the pipe and took a couple of long, slow hits. After about 15 minutes I was fully medicated, seeing everything in a haze. I stared out of the window and looked down at the courtyard. A young couple sat at a table drinking wine; talking… they looked happy. I could see smoke rising from the grill next to them and smelled the scent of barbeque.

Everything I was worrying about started to fade away. The pain in my back turned into a slight annoyance. I smiled a grin ear-to-ear and started beat boxing and singing; doing anything and everything to stop thinking about things – the nightmares from hell that still haunt me.

I poured a glass of cold water from the tap. After slamming a couple, the blue eyes started haunting me again. I felt myself sliding back into the other place when my phone snapped me out of the fall.

I looked at the screen and saw that it was Jessica; I answered annoyingly, "Hello."

"Hi, what are you doing?"

"Just got home from work," I said sharply. "Why, what's up?"

"I don't know; just seeing what you're doing. You never call me just to talk," she said, waiting silently for an answer.

I didn't know what to say. "Sorry, I've just been busy."

"Doing what?"

"Working. You know my hours at work." I got upset. "Is there something you want?"

"Yeah, I was wondering if you would like to come over and eat dinner with me and Aleah tonight and this weekend? You know… have some family time."

I was torn, feeling deep in my heart like I wanted to. But then I start thinking about what had just happened. The pain, the flashbacks, I was afraid to leave the house. I missed my daughter so much but I couldn't drive like this. I lied, "I can't, I have an appointment later today and I have to work this weekend."

"Really? You told me you were off," she said angrily.

"Well Mick asked me to work a couple extra shifts and I said yes." I got upset again. "What do you want me to do about it? I can't just say 'No' now; it's work."

"You never want to spend time with us. Aleah is always asking about you. What should I tell her?"

I felt awful. My heart started to burn.

"I'm sorry, Jessica, but I have to work." I gave in a little, "I can come over after my shift is done. We can eat and play games. You can tell her I have to work and I'll see her later."

"Ok. Whatever," she said.

Then it went silent for a minute.

"How come you don't love me?"

"I never said I didn't."

"Then why did you leave?"

"Because we argue too much."

11

"We argue because you don't even try to listen to anything I have to say and you yell," she said.

"You do too!" I quickly chimed in. "All you do is yell and I can't take it. I don't need people around me yelling all the time. I can't handle it."

"If you loved me you would try."

My gut started hurting. "I do love you, Jessica; I just don't know what to do."

"Talk to me."

Silence fell again, I felt so bad that we couldn't get along. I do love her, but the arguments and fights, yelling in front of Aleah… it was too much. I don't want her to think that is how relationships are. She should have a happy life.

"Ok, Sam! Bye!"

"Tell Aleah I'll call her tonight. I'll see you tomorrow."

"Yep, bye." She hung up, her tone saying all she needed to say.

The room fell quiet. I looked down at the phone and thought of all the good times I've had with them. The times I've curled over laughing when playing with Aleah. Hearing her laughs echoing throughout the house when I tickled her, I loved it… missed it.

How did I get here in this empty apartment, feeling sad and numb inside? I've tried my whole life to feel alive; to feel wanted, to be someone special. I joined the Army because it was where I belonged. Fighting for America, saving lives and making a difference, proving to myself that I could do anything, go anywhere.

Now I'm lost, stuck; sealed away in a cave at the center of a deserted world. I want to feel normal again; feel alive, not numb. My past keeps taking over my mind, flooding it with blood and explosions. I want it to end. I want everything to end.

How did I get here?

It was because of the war. Why did I ever sign up to go in? I don't want to feel like this anymore; alone, struggling to hold onto reality day in and day out. I want a life worth living.

God, what happened to me?

Chapter One: The Beginning

I remember watching the planes blow through the twin towers on CNN. I was watching the television in the corner of my literature class when the screen lit up as the second plane hit; my heart dropped. The entire class went quiet.

We listened as the reporters went back and forth about the carnage that was unfolding. We saw people running for their lives away from the falling debris. People were jumping from the burning buildings and landing on the street. Reporters said that an airplane hit the pentagon, and another one went down over land at the same time as the twin towers.

My God, I felt like the whole thing was just a prank by Hollywood. I even said so, but my teacher said it was real. I was shocked; I've never witnessed anything like it before. It terrified me, the thought of jumping out the side of a building, over a hundred stories high. Who would do something like this? How could this happen in America?

Later that night, reports came out that Al Qaida, some terrorist organization had claimed responsibility for the attacks. It was the first time I heard of a terrorist, let alone a whole organization. I was fuming inside.

How could someone do this? So many innocent people died, for what? I wanted to do something about it. I felt drawn to the military after what I had witnessed that day. I, like so many others, fell victim to the lust for revenge.

Friends in Junior Reserve Officer Training Corps (JROTC) talked about the army all the time. Some of them went to basic training during their junior year in high school. We talked about drills and the training. From what I gathered, it wasn't that much harder than football training.

Dad and I fought for months before I graduated from high school, on what the best plan was. It was my life, but he had a say, to an extent. He initially gave me two options: college or the military. He said he didn't want me still living at his house doing nothing after I graduate. I resented him then, but in hindsight, I should thank him for that.

I wanted to go into college for acting so I could play on Broadway; it was a dream of mine. I played in a couple different productions in school and loved it. My dad, on the other hand, thought I wouldn't make any money and said to be more realistic. The only other thing that I was interested in was the military.

An army recruiter showed up at school one day. I was nervous; half of me wanted to run over and sign up right away, the other half worried if I'd be good enough to make it. Finally I broke the ice and we talked about my options in the service. He said I could go to basic training right away as an enlisted soldier, a private, and work my way up from the bottom. Or, I had the option to go to school for a two-year degree called "college first," then go in as an officer and make more money.

I talked it over with my dad. He didn't like the fact that I wanted to join, which was strange because that's one of the options he gave me, but he did like the thought of my getting an education before joining. So, I decided to go to college first, and signed a contract a month before graduation.

College turned out to be a bad choice, though. I didn't know how to handle it. I partied way too much and skipped class. A lot of the time I was too hung over to get out of bed. I flunked most of my classes the first half of the semester.

On winter break the realization came that I should probably just go into the army. America started accusing Iraq of harboring terrorists and stockpiling weapons of mass destruction. President Bush held press conferences threatening Saddam Husain with military action; maybe even war.

I felt like the military was where I was meant to be, even though my parents didn't want me go. They thought I'd be shipped off to war. I wanted to help though; to do something to help my country. Too many innocent people lost their lives on 9/11. I was ready to serve; to do my part.

It became clear to me that my future was in the army. I called my recruiter and asked him to get me in as soon as possible. I wanted a challenge – to be a soldier for my country.

My recruiter came to me with two options: military police (MP) or medic. My dad suggested that I pick a career to do both in and out of the service. I didn't want be a cop, so MP wasn't even an option. The recruiter told me that the training I'd receive as a medic would help me be a nurse. He said there was a 90 percent chance of being stationed at a hospital too. I thought being a medic would be great. Learning how to save someone's life on the battlefield…something felt powerful about that.

I was sworn into the military on March 3, 2003, with 50 other people. My recruiter picked me up early that morning and drove me to the Military Entrance Processing Station (MEPS). After waiting a few hours, we all filed into a room and were put into formation. There was a podium with the American seal on the front of it. An American flag hung on a pole next to it, swaying slowly from the air vent above it.

A male captain walked into the room dressed in his perfectly pressed class A's. He marched over to the podium and brought us to attention. The officer read a letter from the president of the United States then ordered us to raise our right hand and swore us in.

A tingling heat rushed through my chest at that point. *I'm doing it. I'm actually joining the Army.* I felt proud and super nervous at the same time, knowing that turning back wasn't an option. I didn't want to, but knowing the option wasn't there was unsettling.

I repeated everything the officer said then put my hand down. He congratulated us then handed us over to a sergeant, who led us into a room where we received our orders for basic training.

I knew I was going to be ok no matter where I went; I was in good shape and that was half the battle. The other half was mental, which I had doubts about.

*   *   *

The flight to Oklahoma took just under an hour. I was feeling pretty nervous around a bunch of strangers about to go through the hardest thing in my life. I missed home already.

On the ride to the base my stomach got jittery. I didn't know what to expect. I watched videos about the shark attack; twelve drill sergeants barking at the top of their lungs, spitting and cursing in your face.

When we got there it was much more relaxed than I thought. The drill sergeant that came on our

19

bus to talk was pretty normal and oddly nice. He asked us to follow him and get into formation. He had patience when someone didn't know what to do or if someone wasn't listening. His job was different; not really training us, just prepping us for the torment to come.

The first week was in-processing. We were assigned our dog tags and the gear we needed for training. We also received multiple inoculations and took a physical training test. If you failed the PT test they'd hold you back until you passed; it's called recycling. The military never kicked anyone out for failing the test; they were just forced to work out most of the day until they could pass and go on to the next phase. I'm in good shape, so I wasn't as concerned as some of the other recruits were.

When it came down to the two-mile run, however, I almost didn't pass. It wouldn't have been so hard if I hadn't gotten a shot of penicillin in my ass right before. We lined up on the track, toe to toe on the white line. As soon as the drill sergeant shot the blank, we took off. My cheek was throbbing in pain every time I pushed off with my right foot; my leg started cramping up. I wasn't the only one in pain, though; everyone else was moaning and groaning as they ran too. Halfway around the pain started to fade, giving me the ability to run faster. At least ten people didn't pass. Immediately after the test they had to move all of their gear out of our barracks and into a new one.

On the last day of in-processing, we were marched into an auditorium for a little R&R. We watched Blackhawk Down. It's based on a true story about an Army Ranger battalion who went on a mission into Somalia. They were caught in the shit when heavily armed Somalis shot down two of their Blackhawks.

I remember thinking how crazy it was that so many army rangers died. They were fighting in urban areas with buildings and armed people all around them. I could see that it was hard for them to tell who the enemy was; shit, everyone had a gun.

It would suck to get into a situation like that in war. The movie filled me with anger, the same anger I felt when watching the towers fall. So many U.S. troops were killed in action. That's not how it's supposed to be, we're the good guys. The good guys are supposed to win.

I called my dad after watching the movie. He said he was proud of me that I joined the military, but he also told me he was scared. Bush had declared war against Iraq and he was starting to send troops over. He said I joined at the wrong time. He was scared that he'd lose his only son in war.

I told him not to worry; I could handle anything, even war. I was playing out different scenarios in the back of my mind, fighting enemies in an urban area, like the rangers in Blackhawk Down; running through the streets taking enemy fire, ducking in and out of buildings, taking cover from bullets and exploding rockets. It made me anxious. But all I could do was go through basic training and hope that I learned what I needed to in order to survive.

I told my dad not to worry and we said our goodbyes. I went back to my barracks to pack my bags for the morning.

Chapter Two: Respect

I was awakened in the morning like never before. A tall, dark, muscular drill sergeant burst through the main doors, yelling at the top of his lungs, hitting the side of a metal trash can with a large spoon. *Bang! Bang! Bang! Bang!*

"Get up you filthy privates, GET THE FUCK UP! Formation in 2 minutes downstairs, get up!"

We were all startled, tripping over ourselves trying to get our stuff together. You could hear the drill sergeant counting down the seconds we had left. I ran down the stairs and outside. We all got into formation with our duffel bags on our backs.

The drill sergeant filed us into old rundown brown busses without seats. We stood crunched together as they drove us through the base to our new barracks. We pulled up to a three story, redbrick building. When we came to a stop I saw at least twenty, brown drill sergeant hats through the window, swarming around waiting for us to get off the bus. They were yelling and swearing at the top of their lungs.

"Hurry up, move! Faster! Fucking move it!"

I've never seen anything like it before. It felt like everything we did was wrong. How we walked, how we stood, even the way we looked at them was wrong. As we stood in formation the drill sergeants barked in our faces about anything they could. They taunted us; begged us to hit them or move so they could fuck us up.

One kid yelled at a drill sergeant. With a grim quickness five drill sergeants ran over to him, screaming in his ear, shoving him; getting in his face asking him to try it again. They pushed the guy to the ground and made him do push-ups while they yelled at him; everyone calls it getting smoked. The guy's face turned beet red; it looked like he was about to cry.

It was funny watching him get broke. People yelled at me most of my life, giving me an advantage over most newbies. I also knew none of these guys could hit us; it was all for show. I would probably have had a little more fear if that had not been the case. It made me feel as though all of this was a game just to get under our skin. It was funny to see the guys who fell for it; their faces looking like beets as they pounded it on the pavement, getting screamed at.

A drill sergeant saw me looking over at the kid with a smile on my face. I'm six foot four, two hundred and thirty pounds. The drill had to be around five feet tall and stout. He ran over to me with a little white stool, set it at my feet and stood on it.

"Bend down soldier so I can ask you a question." I bent down a little so we were at eye level.

"What the fuck's so funny private?"

I tried to hold back the laughter building inside.

"Nothing Sergeant, nothing." Something about what I said pissed him off. He screamed at me,

"What the fuck private, who do you think you are, huh? You begin and end each thing you say with 'Drill Sergeant,' you got that?"

"Drill Sergeant, yes Drill Sergeant."

I knew I had a little smirk on my face; I couldn't help it. It was just too funny that he had to stand on a stool.

"Is something funny private?" He barked in my face, breath heavy with coffee and cigarettes.

"Drill Sergeant, No Drill Sergeant!"

"I think something's funny to you. You laughing because I'm so short?" He quickly squinted his right eye and stared at me with the other, wide open.

I couldn't help but burst out in laughter, "No Drill Sergeant."

He snapped on me, pushing me back, jumping off his stool. Three other drill sergeants burst through formation, pushing troops over to get to me. They yelled at me like dogs barking at a wall. I had one in each ear and two in front of me screaming all sorts of shit, spitting in my face.

"You done lost your fucking mind, private! Piece of shit!" One of the drills shoved me again.

I tried responding to the things they were asking but I couldn't get a word out in between all their yelling.

They told me to drop; I fell as quickly as I could. They smoked me just like the other kid; heckling and jeering above me. They were trying to piss me off and it almost worked. That was the whole point of the attack, to break us down and show us who's the boss. I didn't care; I kept it in the front of my mind that I wasn't going to let anyone get to me.

The short drill sergeant told me to get up. I jumped up and snapped to attention, standing straight and stiff, panting heavily and trying to hold still.

"Now, do you understand what's expected of you, private..." he looked down at my nametag, "...Boney?"

"Drill Sergeant, yes Drill Sergeant."

"Good, you better show the same respect to the other drills as you showed me. You got it!"

"Drill Sergeant, yes Drill Sergeant."

My triceps and chest burned from the smoke session. They taunted us for a while before calling us to attention. The head drill sergeant walked through the middle of formation with a harsh look on his face. He stood in front and spoke to us about what's to be expected for the next couple weeks of training. Then he went into introducing all of the drill instructors for our class. There were two for every platoon, four platoons. When he was done they broke us up into platoons.

I was assigned to the Dark Knights. Drill Sergeant Dickens was a big dude; He was the one who woke us up that morning with the trash can. Drill Sergeant Thompson was a middle-aged guy, looked like Jim Carrey. We were assigned bunks immediately after they introduced themselves. First thing they did was lock away our personal bags. The only way we got them back was after graduation. No clothes, no phone, no money. It was the first time I felt my freedom snatched from me.

*   *   *

Every night before lights out we had drill sergeant time. The first night, Drill Sergeant Dickens showed us how to take care of our personal areas. Everything had to be according to regulation.

When we hung our battle dress uniforms in the lockers, they had to be buttoned as if we were wearing them. Our brown T-shirts had to be rolled up tight and six inches long; no shorter, no longer. Our socks and underwear had to be rolled and lined up in a drawer. He gave us two pictures to pass around. Everything had a proper order to it, even our beds.

Pillow up top, blanket and sheet folded a quarter way down the bed; always remembering to fold the bottom ends at a 45-degree angle. When Drill made the bed it was tucked tight with no wrinkles. He bounced a quarter off the top and told us every bed needed to be the same, or there would be hell to pay.

"I'm only warning you this one time, privates. Got it?"

"Hooah Drill Sergeant!" we shouted.

Drill Dickens walked into the sergeants' room and came back out with a black arm patch. The letters PL were stitched to the side in white.

"O'Conner!" he said.

A middle-aged guy with glasses stood up, "Yes Drill Sergeant!"

"You're going to be the platoon leader since you have the highest rank. You're to make sure everyone's accounted for at all times. When I give an order you make sure they follow it. Understood?"

"Yes Drill Sergeant!"

He threw him the patch, "Don't fuck it up or your ass will be demoted. I'll make someone else the PL in a heartbeat."

"Yes Drill Sergeant!"

He looked at everyone, "You privates listen to him like your life depends on it; his word is as good as mine. Got it?"

"Yes Drill Sergeant!"

"Alright make sure everyone gets their shit together before lights out. Dismissed!"

I went over and folded my shirts like he taught us, making sure that I rolled them properly; measuring with a dollar that was being passed around by the PL. He came and checked all of our areas before lights went out.

*   *   *

"You have 1 minute left to eat!" Drill Thompson bellowed in the middle of our dining facility (DEFAC). A couple people sucked their teeth as the sound of silverware clattering on plates filled the room.

I shoved the last two pieces of bacon in my mouth and jumped out of my chair, emptying my tray as I ran outside and took my place in formation. It took me forever to finish the rubbery meat in my mouth. I turned to watch people scramble out of the DEFAC.

Drill Thompson counted down the seconds as he walked outside.

"6, 5, 4…"

"At ease!" We yelled at the top of our lungs as he stepped outside. Our voices echoed through the hallways. A couple guys who were running to their spots stopped abruptly and stood with their hands behind their back.

"Carry on," Drill Thompson said, counting while the rest of the guys jumped into formation. He called us to attention and marched us over towards our company.

As we approached our barracks, the sound of a madman screaming filled the hallway. *What the fuck could that be?* It sounded like Drill Dickens swearing and throwing stuff in our barracks. I looked over to my buddy, private Dillen, a native kid from Wisconsin; we both stared at each other confused.

"Hmm, I wonder what that could be?" Drill Thompson said sarcastically as he stopped us. "Platoon, halt! Right face!" We turned to face him; he gave us a wicked smile.

"I want you troops to go and report to Drill Sergeant Dickens. Fall out!"

I was nervous, what kind of rampage was Drill Dickens on? I ran with everyone up the stairwell into our quarters. We all came to a sudden stop and looked at the room in amazement. The barracks were in shambles. Bunks were pushed over on their sides. Every bed in the room had been flipped over with the bottom spring showing. Mattresses and sheets were scattered around the room. Some of the dressers were knocked over too. I could see Drill Dickens up front still kicking stuff over.

"Fucking privates never do shit right!"

"Dude, what happened?" Dillen said out loud. Drill Sergeant stopped and looked at us panting, sweat dripping down his brow.

"You fucking privates. I showed you fuckers how to make your beds, right?!"

"Yes Drill Sergeant!"

"I came up here to inspect and not one of you had it right. So guess what, I have a fucking present for you, hear you go. You fuckers got 10 minutes to clean this shit up. I'll be back on time and it better be done the right way. Now hurry up!" He kicked the front doors open, stormed out and slammed them shut.

We started flipping over the beds in a mad rush. I grabbed what I thought was my mattress and threw it on top of the bed, along with sheets and a blanket. Then I ran over and helped Killean and a couple other guys pick up.

When we got the beds and dressers up, we started fixing everything according to code. I made my bed just like Drill Sergeant Dickens showed us; it was tight with a 45-degree angle in the corners. I was relieved my dresser stood untouched so I didn't have to worry about it. I gave the other guys a hand with their beds. The second we finished, Drill Dickens walked through the door.

"At ease!" we screamed, standing in position at the foot of our beds. The platoon leader ran over to Drill Dickens and walked with him as he checked our beds. He moved 4 beds down before he started yelling again, "What the fuck is this?" Drill stooped down and pointed at the end of the bed. "Why is this sticking out? HUH!" The PL jumped back as Drill got in his face giving him a cold gaze. "You see this bed, the angles are all fucked up, what the fu-" He balled up his fist; I thought he was going to hit him but he turned around and screamed, "I fucking hate privates!"

Standing on the side of the bed, he squatted down quick then snapped up the bed, flipping it over with one motion, "You lousy fucking privates, fuck! Fu-u-uck!" He yelled fuck with every bed he flipped. He was like a raging bull, destroying everything in his path.

He went down each row until he was done. He made his way back to the front door, kicking it open. He shouted, "You got two minutes to fix this shit."

We scrambled to flip our beds over again, trying to make them properly. The PL went around making sure the fold was at the proper angle and tucked tight.

It didn't take long to get things straight. Drill Dickens walked back in, "At Ease!"

He stood in the front of the room, "Where the fuck is the PL?!" Drill Dickens yelled.

"Here Drill Sergeant," O'Connor screeched, tripping over himself trying to get to him.

"What took you so long, you on fucking vacation?"

"No Drill Sergeant."

"You know what, you're fucking fired! Give me that fucking patch." He reached over and snatched it off his shoulder.

"Reeds!"

"Yes Drill Sergeant!" the tall blonde guy hollered out.

"Get your ass up here, now!" Reeds hurriedly ran up to the front of the room.

"Here, put this on. You're the new PL. Keep fucking track of the time I give you. You're on my time, not on your own." He turned toward us.

"I want every one of you fucking privates on my time. What's the time, Private Reeds?"

Reeds looked at his watch, "0905 hours Drill Sergeant!"

"See," Drill said looking at his watch.

"You're off by a minute, its 0906. I want you privates to set your clocks to 0908 on my mark."

I looked at my watch and adjusted the clock to 0908 then quietly waited.

"Mark!" Drill barked. Beeps filled the room as we set our clocks.

"Come on," Drill Dickens said as he turned and walked down the row with Private Reeds in tow. The time seemed to creep by as he marched down the aisle, carefully inspecting each bed.

When he got to mine, he looked at my bed then quickly looked me in the eye for a minute. He smirked and then walked off. I hadn't noticed that I had stopped breathing, afraid my bed might not be right. I let out a sigh, and wiped the sweat off my brow. I looked down; my brown tee was drenched in sweat.

The further he got down the aisle the more relieved I was; I'm sure everyone felt the same way. We anxiously kept our eyes on him as he finished the inspection.

"About fucking time, Reeds!"

"Hooah, Drill Sergeant!" Reeds confidently cried out.

"I want everyone downstairs in formation for class at 0920 hours. The time is 0915. Is that the time you have, Private Reeds?

"Yes Drill Sergeant!"

"Well fuck. You're on the way to being an outstanding PL private. O'Connor!"

"Yes Drill Sergeant," O'Connor hollered out.

"You should take some lessons from Private Reeds here on being a better PL. Got it!"

"Yes Drill Sergeant," O'Connor mumbled, more quiet than the last.

"I'll see you privates downstairs."

"At ease," we bellowed as he walked out the door.

"Carry the fuck on." He left, slamming the door shut. I rushed over to my locker and grabbed my pen and notepad for taking notes.

"Ok!" Reeds said, "We have to get downstairs. Three minutes left, hurry up!" I bolted towards the door and ran downstairs, jumping into formation as Drills Thompson and Dickens walked out of headquarters (HQ).

"At ease!"

Chapter Three: Order and Chaos

Private Bricks was on fireguard duty, a tall lanky guy who liked to crack jokes and goof off when Drill Sergeant's back was turned. Everyone had to take turns on guard at night, watching the barracks and reporting to the drill sergeant on duty every hour. Drill Dickens liked to poke at him every now and then because they're both from Alabama.

I was tired from marching around doing drills all day, everyone was. I couldn't wait to get in bed and relax my muscles. Bricks was standing in the front of the room sleepy-eyed when he turned the lights out at 2100 hours. It didn't take me long to pass out from exhaustion.

In the middle of the night I was startled awake by shouting. The lights flicked on, stinging my eyes as they opened; everything was blurry. It took me a second to realize I was in the barracks.

Drill Dickens was yelling at the top of his lungs, "Get the fuck up! What the fuck is this shit?! Everyone up now!"

Rushing to the foot of my bed, I stood at ease with everyone else wondering what was going on.

Drill Dickens swiftly marched down the aisle with a furious look on his face. Private Bricks was stumbling along behind him.

"It seems like Private Bricks here doesn't like to follow the fucking rules, do you Bricks?" He stopped and turned towards him. Bricks tried saying something but Drill Dickens got in his face.

"You shut the fuck up when I'm talking." It looked like Drill wanted to fight. His chest bulged with his hand pointed in Bricks' face. Drill turned back around.

"It seems like Private Bricks here likes to sleep when he's supposed to be on fire guard. What do you think, you're special?!" he said, getting back in his face.

"Half-right face" Drill yelled. Everyone turned. "Front leaning rest position move!"

We dropped down in the push up position. *Fuck man, why did he have to fall asleep, I'm dead tired.* I was still aching from yesterday. My shoulders and arms burned, threatening to give out.

"Down, up, down, up!" Drill Sergeant bellowed, as we beat our face over and over again on the ground. I managed to get a look at my watch; it was two in the morning.

"Halfway-down! UP! Halfway down, burn!" I went down to the ground then halfway up, repeating it over and over again. My arms cramped up, I couldn't hold myself up anymore. It felt like a weight was pulling me to the ground, so I dropped.

"Private Boney get your ass up. Start pushing!" Drill shouted.

Reluctantly, I pushed myself up, straining out loud, "U-u-ah!" My arms wobbled like rubber. It felt like all we did was get smoked day and night; I never got rest. I tried my best to keep pushing, but it was painful.

Thirty minutes past and Drill Dickens had it steaming in the room. The windows were fogged up from the heat and sweat that poured out of our skin. I looked around the room to see Privates Bauer and O'Conner drenched like me. Looking down I noticed a pool of sweat gathering on the ground as it dripped off my face.

"Position of attention move!"

We all snapped up and stood still with fists at our sides panting feverishly.

"Everyone thank Private Bricks for falling asleep and waking you up."

"Thank you Private Bricks!" We shouted, some louder than others. I could hear a number of people quietly swearing at him.

"Everyone get the fuck back to bed! Lights out!"

We quickly hopped back into our beds. "Now." Drill got in Brick's face; mouth inches from his eyes, "Don't you fall back to sleep you piece of shit. You better report to me on time. You got it!"

"Yes Drill Sergeant," he mumbled.

Drill turned off the lights and walked out. A couple of the guys quietly cursed at Bricks.

"You fucking prick!"

"Lazy ass!"

He stood at the front of the room slouched over, looking tired and worn. Felt bad for the guy, but I was pissed too. Covered in sweat, sheets sticking to my arms; it sucked.

*   *   *

"Get up! Get up, five minutes before formation," Drill Thompson barked from the front of the room. I jumped up and quickly made my bed. I snatched my sneakers off my locker and grabbed my neon reflective belt; putting it around my waist as I ran downstairs.

The bugle started playing "Reveille." The company commander cried out, "Company, attention! Present arms!" We all saluted. I was used to the routine by now; getting up early to salute a flag I couldn't see while swaying back and forth trying to stay awake.

When it ended the commander handed us off to the drills for morning physical training (PT). We broke up into different groups according to speed. A group was the fastest; C had a bunch of overweight and out of shape guys. I fell in with B group, right in the middle.

The drill that led B group always ran fast though; we kept up with A group most mornings. After running two miles we jogged back to the company quarters to get smoked for a half hour before being released.

I was tired; beat up. Sweat ran down my arms from my soaked shirt. I had grass and dirt smeared all over my arms and legs. I walked over to my locker, undressed, and grabbed my hygiene bag; I could feel the hot water running over my head already.

It usually took a while for a turn in the shower. There were only seven showers and thirty-five of us. We quickly washed, knowing the thirty minutes we had were ticking away before breakfast formation.

After a disappointingly cold shower, I hurried and got my green camouflage battle dress uniform (BDU) on and ran downstairs. Before we marched out, Drill Thompson gave us a warning: "No candy, soda, or sweets of any kind; same as always. If me, or any other drill sees someone with that shit, all of you are paying. Understood?"

"Yes Drill Sergeant!"

"Good. Platoon attention! Right face! Forward march! You're left...left...left, right."

At dinner last night, private Bricks took it upon himself to grab a piece of cake when the drill sergeants' backs were turned. As he stuffed his face three drills ran over to him. They forced him to spit it out and told him to get out of the DEFAC. We got smoked for hours because of him.

We stopped outside of the DEFAC. The National Guard and Reservists were told to go to the front of the line. *Every time, shit.* For some reason they received special treatment. Some of them walked to the front of formation with smug looks on their faces. My stomach growled as they passed. I hunched over in pain, angry that I never go first. I was always stuck, slowly filing into the door smelling the food that was feet away. I could literally have a conversation with my stomach it growled so much.

I grabbed my tray and went down the line, telling the lunch ladies what I wanted, giving them a huge smile to try and get extra scoops. I grabbed a milk carton and sat down at a table.

The drills sat in the corner of the room to eat. Two drills were always walking around watching us, waiting to jump if we messed up. We held our heads down while we ate and we couldn't talk. I swear at times it felt like I was stuck in prison. I got a couple bites of egg in my stomach before Drill Brown started cussing in his southern accent.

"What the fuck is you doing private! What are the rules, huh? No fucking talking right?" I looked over to see him pointing his hand in Baker's face.

"Private Baker! You causing trouble again opening your fucking mouth?" Drill Thompson screamed, rushing past me to get to Baker.

"What the hell is your problem?" he barked at him, spitting in his face when he talked. Baker just stared down at his plate looking distant.

"Ok, you have exactly one minute to eat the rest of your fucking food." He looked around at everyone.

"Fuck it! All the Dark Knights, you have one minute. One fucking minute to eat the rest of your food and get the fuck out to formation."

Damn, not again. A bunch of people sucked their teeth; we couldn't get a full meal in without someone fucking it up. It always seemed like Baker was the cause of it. I shook my head, *when will he learn.* I shoveled food in my mouth chewing as quickly as I could, swallowing pieces of pancake whole.

Clanking of silverware on plates filled the room as Drill Thompson started counting down the seconds. I got most of my food down by the time he got to twenty. I took a swig of milk, jumped up and dumped my tray and bolted outside. Drill Thompson walked out counting down.

"Three, two, one…" He finished his count as a couple people were struggling to get in their spots.

Drill Thompson got pissed, "Ok. You fucking want to take your time!" He called us to attention. "Half-left face." *Fuck, we just ate* was all I could think.

"Front leaning rest position move." We dropped, some faster than others. Drill counted off as we beat our face.

"Flutter kick position move." We all flipped to our backs. I put my legs straight, lifted them up six inches and started to kick.

"One, two, three"

"ONE!"

"One, Two, Three"

"TWO!"

My stomach started cramping up. I think I ate too much. All of a sudden I heard a guy start puking. Drill snapped again.

"Private Roberts, get the fuck up and clean it now!" Drill was in his face steaming mad, "I want this pad fucking sparkling. Who said you could throw up here? Hurry the fuck up!"

He ran over to the latrine and came out with a wad of paper towels in his hand. He stooped down and started scooping it up. It was getting all over his hands. The drill kept at him, in his face, while we were in push-up position,

"Hurry up you fucking maggot! You're making everyone wait for you! Get it up!"

Roberts rushed past me and threw the shit in the trashcan. I could smell the puke on him as he passed, dropping back on the ground in his spot.

"Position of attention, move," Thompson said.

"You need to keep your fucking mouths shut and eat your fucking food. Next time you won't get any time to finish eating. What do I care; I get to eat my food with or without you fucking troops. You got it?"

"Yes Drill Sergeant!"

"Good. Right face!"

We all ran up to the barracks when we were released, to grab our gear. I was behind Roberts going up, he smelled bad. He went into the restroom with a pouty look on his face. It was kind of funny, I'm just glad it wasn't me. Thank God for my iron stomach.

*   *   *

"Fucking Baker!" Drill Sergeant Thompson snatched Baker out of formation by the collar of his shirt while we were doing rifle drills.

"Platoon! Half-left face! Front-leaning rest position move!" Drill Thompson shouted. We got down placing our rifles on the tops of our hands.

"What the fuck is wrong with you? Why can't you do a left turn correctly? Every time I look at you you're tripping over your feet. Do you have a fucking problem? You act like you have two left fucking feet."

"No, Drill Sergeant! Just a little tired Drill Sergeant!" Baker mumbled.

We all sucked our teeth. It's been like this most of the day with this kid. We were in class watching a video and he kept falling asleep. I admit, sitting in a warm room watching training videos makes me pretty damn tired too, but this was crazy. He didn't have any rhythm, tripping over his feet every five minutes. We're always being smoked because of him.

"Well since you're so tired you can stand here with me and take a break while everyone else suffers because of your laziness." He said coldly.

He started shouting, "One, Two, Three!"

"One!" we yelled, doing push-ups in cadence.

"One, Two, Three!"

"Two!"

I was tiredly counting off while staring straight at Baker.

"One, two, three!"

"Nine!"

"Eat your milk and cookies!"

"Ten"

"They taste so good."

"Eleven"

Marching drills were no joke. Mess up once and the Drill made everyone pay. It was easy for me to pick up marching; I had rhythm. But there were some guys like Baker who didn't have a lick of it. Everyone was pissed off at him.

"One, two, three," he said an octave higher.

"Halt," we all sounded off as loud as we could.

"Alright Private Baker, let's see if you can fucking get in the right step. You're such a fuck up you know that? Get your head out of your ass and stop making everyone else pay for your shit. Everyone thank Private Baker."

"Thank you Private Baker," we shouted.

"Position of attention move!"

We jumped back up with our dummy rifles in hand. Baker ran back in line. I could see he was tired of doing this over and over again.

"Forward, march!" We stepped off with our left foot, marching relentlessly to the cadence from Drill Thompson.

"Your left, left, left, right."

After lunch we marched back over to the command post (CP). We filed in one by one to put away our dummy rifles. Drill Thompson released us to grab our necessary gear for map reading and land navigation. I rushed upstairs and headed straight to the latrine to take a piss. While peeing I heard a guy scream followed by a soft thud.

"What the fuck is he doing?" someone asked.

I hurried out of the stall and ran over to a bunch of guys stooped over in front of a window, looking outside.

Dillen cupped his hands over his mouth, "Holy shit dude, he jumped," he called out, jumping back with a huge smile on his face. "He actually had the balls to do it, damn."

When I looked out, Private Baker was on the ground with his leg awkwardly bent next him. He was screaming. "OW! Fuck! Fuck!"

Drill Thompson calmly walked over to him, screaming at the top of his lungs, "What the fuck is this! What the fuck are you doing Baker! Get up! What's wrong with you?"

"Ahh! I can't!" Baker cried out.

"He jumped!" Private Bauer yelled out the window. Drill Thompson looked up at us, then down at Baker.

"What the fuck?" He barked, "Now I've got to deal with your shit Baker, you fucking pussy!

We started laughing. I couldn't believe what I was hearing; he didn't care about him one bit.

Drill pointed at Baker, "Stay here." He walked into the HQ and slammed the door behind him.

"Where the fuck is he going to go, Sergeant?" Bauer joked. We all chuckled.

"Why the fuck would he do that?" I asked.

"Probably trying to get out on Section 8," said Bauer.

"What's that?" I asked, totally clueless.

"It's pretty much the only way you can get out of the military with an honorable discharge. It's for crazies; people who are mentally insane."

"Never knew that. That's fucking stupid though. Why wouldn't he just try to stick it out. What a pussy. Who tries to kill themselves?" I didn't get it; basic hasn't been extremely hard. I couldn't imagine trying to kill myself just to get out.

"He wouldn't have made it anyway. He's a fuck up and a pussy," said Dillen angrily.

"I'm glad he jumped, at least now we can do drills without getting smoked," Miller said jokingly. We all laughed.

I looked at my watch and got anxious, "We've got 3 minutes to get downstairs. Let's go."

I grabbed my gear and ran downstairs. I hopped in formation and looked over to Baker. There were medics surrounding him. One person was putting his leg in a splint.

Drill Thompson walked back out of the office.

"At ease!"

Our voices echoed off the walls as we snapped our arms behind us.

"Carry on," Drill Thompson said irritated with a livid look on his face.

He walked over to Baker cursing under his breath.

"Once you're done at the hospital you can come see me, you fucking idiot," he said.

Private Baker was on a litter by then, shaking his head, moaning hysterically. The medics lifted him up and walked off.

Drill Thompson marched to the front of formation and called us to attention. Then put us at ease.

"For any of you little shits that want to pull a stunt like that, go ahead! I don't care. Kill yourself." He looked around at us, taking a moment for it to sink in. I didn't expect a lecture on killing myself. I was blown away by how blunt and serious he was.

"If you want to die so bad, you might as well. Last year I had a cadet who was going through some family shit. One day I was walking over from the DEFAC and saw this fucker jump off of a two-story building. When I got to him, people were crowding all around. He was crying on the ground, fussing about how much he didn't want to be alive. He said he wished that he was dead. I told him that next time, he should jump head first, if he really wants to die so bad." I was shocked. At that moment I thought Drill Thompson was nuts.

"Three days later I'm walking through the CP when I hear an ambulance. I see people standing around a body on the ground. It was that same troop lying on the ground in a pool of blood." He stopped for a minute and stared at us.

"He took my advice. If you really want to go, you might as well do it the right way so you're not a problem for other people." He stared at us again, his face turning red with anger.

"Now I have to write up paperwork and shit because of that asshole. Sorry piece of shit." He looked over to where Baker was; he shook his head and yelled, "Platoon attention! Right face. Forward march! Your left, left, left right."

Chapter 4: Gas, Gas, Gas

I grabbed my rucksack and started organizing my gear. Drill Thompson wrote a list on the board of what we needed to pack. Sergeant's time was spent going over plans for tomorrow: a 6-kilometer road march to the gas chamber, where we'd be forced to inhale pepper gas.

I was tense. My stomach turned when I thought about it. I'd seen videos on the Internet when researching basic. Soldiers marched in the chamber row by row with their masks on; next they came running out with snot and drool pouring out, coughing hysterically; waving their hands wildly around like their life depended on it.

The PL was making his way around the room inspecting bags, making sure we had the correct items. It was O'Conner again; for some reason the drills took a liking to the guy. They said it was because he had seniority in rank; he was the oldest guy in our platoon. I hadn't had a problem with him; he was actually pretty fair when it came to decision making.

I placed my gear on the bed as he called off items on the checklist. After checking the seal on my gas mask, he cleared me and moved on to Brown.

I changed into my PT clothes and brought my boots and polishing gear downstairs. Dillen was sitting on the ground with Johnson and Bauer so I joined them.

"What the fuck Boney?" Johnson said in his best Drill Thompson voice that I laughed, "Shut up, dude. I'm tired of hearing him already. It haunts me in my sleep."

"Hell yeah, I know." said Dillen, "I wish I could punch him in his fire marshal Bill looking face!" he jabbed the air a few times with his fists. We laughed silently, trying not to draw any unwanted attention.

"At ease!" a couple troops shouted.

I dropped everything and shot up locking my hands behind me. Drill Thompson had walked out of the headquarters office. He looked around for a couple seconds checking if everyone was standing.

"Carry on," he said, walking away.

Dillen jumped at him after he walked by. I sat down and started polishing my boots.

"You nervous about the gas chamber?" Johnson asked.

"Nope" I said, "I'm not scared, I just want to get it over with."

"Same here," said Dillen, "I don't give a fuck, bring it on!" he slapped his chest. "Can't be that bad if everyone has to do it".

"Ok, we'll see how much snot is pouring out of your nose when you come out crying" Bauer said, rubbing his eyes with his fists, "whining like a baby, Whaa-"

Dillen punched him on the arm "Ha, Ha funny. Ok baby face, we'll see who's shitting their diapers when we go through."

*   *   *

"Get up! Wake up! You've got 15 minutes before formation. Get up!" Drill Dickens shouted at the front of the room. I sprang out of bed and ran to the latrine to quickly shave my face and brush my teeth. I threw my rucksack on and strapped my gas mask securely around my waist before rushing downstairs with the rest of the platoon.

It was still dark out. Everyone was bathed in orange from the lights on the walls as they stood silently in formation with their gear neatly placed on the ground at their feet. I ran to my spot and followed suit, shivering as a cold breeze blew through.

It looked like everyone in the company was down on the platform waiting for orders. All of sudden the HQ doors flew open as the drill sergeants came marching out.

"At ease," we yelled, everyone silent as they walked to their platoons. Drill Thompson stopped at the front of formation.

"Ok, listen up. The lovely ladies at the DEFAC decided they were going to open the doors early for us to have warm chow before we head out this morning." he said disturbingly calm.

"We're going to march over to the chow hall and eat quickly so we can get a move on."

I felt good that we didn't have to eat Meals Ready to Eat (MRE) for breakfast; nice hot chow was always better than MRE's from a pouch.

Drill Thompson marched us over to the chow hall where we all ate quickly and quietly. We marched back over to the CQ, put our gear on, then stood silently.

Drill Dickens opened up the storage room and filed us in one by one to get a dummy rifle to march with. When everyone was back in formation Drill Thompson screamed, "Gas, Gas, Gas." He threw a metal canister into formation engulfing us in a cloud of smoke.

I stopped breathing and tore my mask out of the bag on my hip. I set the butt of my rifle on the ground leaning it against my leg and quickly strapped the mask over my face. I placed my hand over the canister and took a breath in making sure it had a proper seal before tightening the straps and threw the hood over my head. Picking up my rifle, I looked around at everyone else to see two people struggling with their masks.

"Private Johnson! You having a fucking problem?" said Drill Thompson, moving to stand in front of him.

"The seal Drill Sergeant, it won't seal properly." He sounded panicked.

"Let me fucking see." Drill Thompson grabbed the mask from him and checked the straps.

"Let me see you put it on."

He tried it again. Sergeant Thompson took it from him again and looked inside.

"It's too fucking small for your face. Why didn't you say something before, Private?"

"It fit before Drill Sergeant!"

"Well then it's just going to have to fit until we get back from our trip today. You have to take your mask off in the chamber anyway. Maybe next time you'll pay closer attention to your gear. If this was a real attack, you'd be dead," Thompson said angrily.

He shoved the mask in Johnson's chest.

"Do any more of you shitheads have problems with your mask?" Everyone stood silent.

"Good. All clear, all clear."

I took off my mask and folded it back up, storing it securely in its bag. Drill Thompson put his gear on and stood at the front.

"Ok privates, let's move out!" he called us to attention and marched us out to the road.

We got into single file and marched down the side of the paved road. Drill Dickens was in the front leading us with Thompson in the back.

We silently marched around base; the only sound was from our boots hitting the pavement and metal clanking from the buckles on our gear. As the sun rose, Drill Dickens led us off onto a dirt road, immediately picking up the pace to a fast walk; I was nearly running to keep up with him. People kept stopping from exhaustion; whining about how they couldn't keep up. As I ran past them to quickly close the gap, Drill Thompson came up to push them forward; shoving their pack screaming, "Keep fucking moving!" Eventually, 10 other guys and I were the only ones in line behind Dickens; the other guys were scattered yards behind, struggling to keep up.

Close to the afternoon we came to an old brick building off the side of the road. Drill Dickens stopped in an open area and dropped his rucksack. We marched over to him and lined up in formation.

"Take off your gear and set it neatly in front of you while we wait for the stragglers." Dickens said, quickly yelling, "Drink water!"

We tiredly cried out, "Hydrate or die, Drill Sergeant. Hydrate or die."

After setting my gear down I started guzzling my water out of my canteen trying to satisfy an unquenchable thirst. The sun was bearing down on us, making it hard to cool down. I poured water over my head, watching the rest of the platoon trickle in.

Suddenly I heard a crack and a loud hissing sound. "Gas, gas, gas!" Drill Thompson yelled throwing a can into formation. I held my breath and quickly put my mask on as smoke started creeping towards me. Drill Thompson watched us from the side of formation making sure we all got our masks on.

"Ok, good. You all survived." Thompson said, "From here on, you keep that mask on until you're told to take it off. You will be filed in by rows. When instructed to take off your masks, you're expected to say your full name, social security number and date of birth. If you don't talk or breathe, you will be forced to. One way or another everyone will get a nice big dose of gas today. Understood?"

"Yes Drill Sergeant!" We all sounded muffled from the masks.

"Good! I will start filing you in row by row in a couple minutes."

Drill Thompson put on his mask and walked into the building. A minute later he walked out and filed in the first row. I was glad to be in the second row; I hated going first. I was struggling to take a deep breath with the mask on. I was nervous, not knowing what to expect. A couple minutes went past before Drill Thompson walked out in a cloud of fumes.

"Next group!" he said with a muffled voice.

We filed into the building with our hands on each other's shoulder. The gas was so thick I couldn't see the guy in front of me. My skin started burning as we crept deeper into the building. We stopped in a lit room where a couple drill sergeants were standing. I could see one of the drills messing with a disk on top of a tray; smoky fumes were pouring into the air.

It was hard to tell who the drills were until the drill in the front started talking. I could tell from the harsh deep voice that it was Drill Dickens.

"Alright you fucking privates, we're going to do this quick so we can get the next group in."

He walked up to Bauer. "Take off your mask!"

Bauer took it off and immediately started coughing. He slouched over in a coughing fit but Drill Dickens pushed him up.

"Name!" he barked.

"Davi- cough, cough. Bauer 356 234 cough, cough. Augh- man it burns," he said, struggling to breathe.

Drill Dickens let him go and moved over to me. I watched as he ran out the door with his arms raised.

"Mask off!" Dickens yelled. I ripped off my mask and immediately felt burning all over my face and eyes.

"Go ahead."

"Samuel bone- cough, cough, cough. 469 cough." I had snot running down my face. It felt like a hundred bees were stinging me in the eyes. Every breath I tried taking was painful; it felt like breathing in fire. Tears were pouring down my face making my skin burn worse. I heard Drill Dickens chuckle. "Ok, go."

I walked as quickly as I could toward the door; all I could see through my burning eyes was light pouring through the smoke. A drill sergeant by the door guided me: "This way. This way." When he opened the door he said, "Wave your arms to get the smoke out."

I ran out towards the light, feeling the cool air hit my face as I gasped to breathe. I started whipping my arms around, spitting on the ground, trying anything that was within my power to get rid of the burning. I wiped the snot and drool from my face with my sleeves; *God that was awful*.

It took a couple minutes for my eyes to stop watering, they were burning so bad. I thought if it was this bad from pepper gas, it must be ten times worse with the real thing. That would be a cruel way to die.

I walked over to my gear, listening to the first group of guys laughing hysterically. Dillen came running out with a huge snot string dripping out of his nose. He started spitting like I did, over and over again. I couldn't help but to laugh a bit, thinking about what my face might have looked like.

Chapter 5: Weapons

"This," Drill Dickens said, holding up a black rifle, "is an M16 semi-automatic rifle."

He had a smile on his face, chew in his lower lip. We were gathered outside his office in our barracks for sergeant time.

"You fucking privates are all moving into white phase tomorrow. You made it to weapons training. Congratulations."

"Yes!" we cheered, only to have Drill Dickens shout at us, "Who the fuck told you could talk! Huh! Shut the fuck up when I'm talking, shit!" We went dead silent afraid of a smoke session.

"Now, I'm going to teach you how to use your weapon effectively in the line of fire. Listen up while I explain every part of this rifle. This weapon will be a part of you just as much as your arm is."

He taught us how to disassemble the rifle and how to clean it. He went on to explain how we adjusted the scope. I had never fired a weapon before, so I paid close attention to every word he said.

The first three days of the white phase were spent practicing on paper targets, adjusting our scopes and learning how to fire in different positions. We also practiced a breathing technique that helped steady our weapon. It was a lot to pick up, but I was quick to learn.

We were all assigned our rifles the morning of our live fire test and filed into brown buses parked next to our barracks. It took us 15 minutes to drive to the range. It was huge. There were 14 different firing pits along the line. A tall, tan building stood in the middle with speakers on each side. Dirt and grass mounds were spread out in 50-meter increments down range; black silhouettes riddled with bullet holes sat high on each.

A tall, stocky man walked out of the watchtower and down the stairs. He had on blue jeans and a white T-shirt with his beer belly sticking out.

Drill Thompson called everyone to attention, then went over the rules of the firing range. "I don't want to see any weapons pointed anywhere except down range. You will get your ammo at the ammo point when your name is called. Those of you who aren't testing will sit in the bleachers silently, until your name is called. Understood?"

"Yes Drill Sergeant!" we shouted.

Testing went in alphabetical order. I started working on my breathing technique, taking deep breaths in and letting it out pretending to squeeze the trigger as I took down an imaginary target. I kept repeating it trying to keep myself busy to drown out my nerves.

Sergeant Dickens voice cut through my thoughts, "Barnes, Baker, Bauer, Boney..." My heart jumped as he said my name. I sprang up with my weapon and ran over to him jumping into a single file line. He marched us over to the ammo point, filing us through to grab two full magazines for our test. We waited quietly in line while the first round of troops finished.

The guy in the tower called out on the loudspeaker, "Green to go."

"All right privates," Sergeant Dickens chimed in.

"Get into your positions. Don't load the magazines. I repeat, don't load your weapons until they give the go ahead."

We walked down the firing range in line; I stopped at pit number 8 and climbed down; placing my magazines on the ground next to me and pointed my rifle down range.

The drills walked up and down the range watching us closely. Pit number 9 was empty, but Drill Dickens climbed in right before the loud speaker told us to load up.

Dickens yelled over to me, "Hey private," I looked back at him, "What the fuck you know about shooting? I bet I'll hit more fucking targets than you." He smirked at me, "You look nervous."

"No Drill Sergeant, just lucky I have a chance to beat you." I smirked back at him.

"What the fuck you say to me private?" He tried looking serious, doing his best not to smile. He spit on the ground.

"Ok, mister big and bad Boner-r-r." he said annoyingly, "I'm gonna show you the fuck up." He loaded his chamber; I turned and did the same.

"Keep your fucking weapon down range!" He yelled at me obnoxiously. I had it down range; fucker was trying to spook me.

"Yes Drill Sergeant." I flipped him off so he couldn't see it. I tried calming myself while placing my rifle into my shoulder.

I stared downrange through my scope with both my eyes. I used my right eye to aim and my left to scope out targets. We're trained to see better this way.

The lights on a pole downrange slowly counted down from red to yellow to green; a target popped up behind a dirt mound 50 meters in front of me. It was a black silhouette of a head and shoulders; I fired. It went down and another target popped up about 150 yards out. I fired and knocked it down. I felt like celebrating, I was doing so well.

The targets kept popping up and I kept knocking them down. A 300-yard target popped up. It felt like forever before I got a good aim. I took a breath in and as I let it out I stopped halfway and fired. The target fell. "Hell yeah," I mumbled under my breath. I was actually good at this.

"Good shot; I bet you won't do it again," Drill Dickens yelled.

I took out another target 200 yards out before the 300-yard one popped back up again. Aiming carefully on center mass, I breathed and fired. The target didn't go down. I got mad, swearing under my breath; I could hear Drill Dickens laughing off to my side.

After a couple more, the loudspeaker rang. That was our cue to unload our weapons and jump out of the pit to prepare for the second round of the test.

"Guess who got a perfect score?" Drill Dickens said, grinning at me. All I could do was smile back, wanting to tell him to fuck off. I dropped back down into the prone position, and aimed my weapon downrange leaning on my elbows, trying to make sure I was straight.

The guy in the tower told us to load our weapons. I popped my magazine in and loaded the chamber. I turned to rag on Drill Dickens, when I felt a sudden rush of air sweep over me; something hit me in the side. "Ow!" I hollered, grabbing my ribs, "What the fuck?"

I heard someone yell off to my left, "No you fucking don't!"

I looked over to see Drill Dickens kick a rifle out of Private Bauer's hand; he had the barrel pointed at his chest. Dickens snatched him up off the ground with one sweep of his arms, throwing him back off the range. Bauer stumbled and fell back, rolling across the ground.

"What the fuck are you doing, you piece of shit!" Drills Thompson and Dickens snatched him off of the ground by his collar, forcing him to stand.

"You stupid fucking kid," Drill Thompson barked in his face, "Trying to kill yourself?" Bauer fell back to the ground and cried. The Drills put him in handcuffs and dragged him off to the side. He sat on the ground red faced, bawling like a baby.

The watchtower instructed us to unload our magazines. I lay on my stomach watching the Drills rag on Bauer as they dragged him off the range; amazed at the balls he had trying to kill himself with his M16. I couldn't figure out what would bring so many people to try and commit suicide. The option of suicide, instead of war, wasn't even a choice for me, I wanted to be in the army; I guess that was the difference between us.

*　　　　　*　　　　　*

"Grenade!" I yelled, pulling the pin out of the baseball sized explosive, letting the clip fly. I threw it hard down range then jumped back behind the wall with Drill Sergeant Drake and started counting. "One, two, three, four, five..." *Boom*!

A couple seconds and I felt the ground shake from the blast. I was surprised at how heavy the grenade was compared to the dummies. It took a lot of force to throw it downrange. After Drill Drake passed me I took off running toward the bunker behind us and waited with the rest of the group to move to the next station. I watched the group ahead of us take turns firing orange dummy rounds with the grenade launcher into blown out cars and busses. When the last guy finished, Sergeant Drake began walking over to us. We ran outside and lined up.

"Ok you all passed this station," Sergeant Drake said, stopping in front of the group; "Good work."

He pulled Johnson out of line. "Private Johnson here is going to march you soldiers over to the next course for grenade launcher testing."

"Yes Drill Sergeant!" we collectively yelled.

"Alright. Move out," Sergeant Drake ordered, quickly pivoting on his heel to walk away.

Johnson marched us over to the grenade launcher course. He stopped us in front of trainer Drill Baker. He told us to fall out.

"Take a seat soldiers, I want to make sure you can all see me." We sat in a half circle around him.

"This," he held up a black tubular weapon, "is an M203 grenade launcher. This weapon can create a lot of damage if used correctly. In fact all the weapons you use today may one day save your life, if used correctly."

He had a stern look on his face. He went into explaining the different grenade rounds, using pictures on a white board for visuals.

"There are smoke grenades with various colors that you can use to either mark an area for extraction or to blind the enemy of your movements."

He pointed to another round "This is your common high explosive round, also called a Frag. Use this for a heavy assault on your enemy; exceptional for clearing buildings. They are highly effective."

He set the board down and picked up a grenade round with a light blue tip. "Today you will be practicing with the dummy round. The first step is to open the chamber." He clicked open the chamber and pushed it forward.

"Then all you do is stick it in the tube like so, with the tip facing forward." He slid the round in and closed the chamber.

"All you need to do is take aim through the sights and pull the trigger." Drill Baker walked up to the range and flipped up the sight. He took aim and pulled the trigger. It flung out with a *Thunk!* A bright orange round launched out and stuck into the side of a blown out bus. It burned for a couple seconds before going out.

"Perfect aim. Ok, Private Johnson, you're up first."

Johnson stood up and walked over to drill. He fired off a round, but barely came close to the target. A couple guys cracked jokes and laughed.

After Dillen took his turn, I walked up and grabbed the M203 from Drill Sergeant; it was lighter than I expected. I shifted it back and forth in my hand.

"I want you to take out that bus soldier," he said, pointing to a burnt out school bus, lying crooked on bare axles.

"Roger Sergeant."

I loaded a round into the chamber and took aim through the sights. I tilted the weapon back, taking aim at the bus through the 150 yard mark and pulled the trigger.

Thunk! The round flew out and stuck on the side of the bus.

"Hmmm, you might just be a natural, Private Boney," Drill said to me. "Next!"

Chapter 6: Storms

It was dark and raining heavily. Even though I had a parka on, I was drenched from head to toe. We had been on a road march since late that afternoon – our last one on the way to the final field training exercise. I moved fast, trying to keep the pace, with my feet sloshing around in my shoe.

Drill Thompson led us into a wooded area. We came to a clearing where he brought us back into formation. It began thundering and lightning like crazy; the wind was blowing strong enough that I had to struggle to not be blown over.

Drill Thompson yelled over the wind "Alright! This is where we're going to set up base operations!"

"I want you men to set up a perimeter and dig out trenches where we will guard our position. After we get that completed, you'll take turns setting up tents for the night. Each one of you will take turns on guard duty tonight. Is that understood?"

"Yes Drill Sergeant."

"Ok. Fall out and get to work."

We spread out, making a large circle around the clearing. My position had a clear view of an open field across from us. I took my gear, unfolded my shovel and started digging out a trench. After a minute of clawing away at the ground I noticed that there were far more rocks than dirt; every time I hit the ground the shovel vibrated in my hands. I kept pounding away, knowing I couldn't give up until I could stick my body in the ground. Everyone else was having just as much trouble. All I heard was thunder mixed with clanking and cussing.

"Fucking ground. Shit!" Dillen screamed out, stabbing the ground as hard as he could.

After an hour of digging, my trench was only 6 inches deep. Drill Thompson made everyone stop. We started taking guard shifts and set up our tents for the operation. Dillen was my "battle buddy" so he took first watch.

My hands were throbbing sore and freezing cold from digging. My hands were burning the whole time I put my tent up. Dickens ordered everyone to set up the large tents for operation. It had stopped raining by the time we were done.

I hurried and changed into dry clothes then walked over to Dillen to switch out. He was asleep in the prone position with his head on his rifle so it looked like he was awake. I kicked his boot and whispered "Dude, get the fuck up."

"What?" He yelped, jumping awake.

"Switch out."

"I'm fucking drained," he said, standing up to stretch.

"Yeah, join the club bro."

I got down in my trench and looked out into the field. I was cold and tired. It took everything I had to fight off the sleep I was longing for.

The wind started picking up, blowing harder than before. Out over the field I saw lightning bolts shoot down across the sky over and over again.

"What the fuck!" one of the guys screamed. "There's a tornado!" I scanned the field trying to see what he was bitching about. I couldn't make out anything other than lightening and dark clouds.

A couple guys got out of their positions and ran back to the drill sergeants' tent yelling, "Tornado, Drill Sergeant, there's a tornado!"

When I turned back around, a grey and black swirling blob slowly twisted its way across the field. Lighting kept shooting through the sky, illuminating it, making it feel like my brain was taking mental pictures.

"Holy shit," I whispered, "Shit!"

My body started shivering; I wanted to get up and run, but the drills hadn't ordered us to.

Both Thompson and Dickens yelled behind me. "Get the fuck back to your positions! Who told you to fucking leave your post! Get back down there!"

They were pushing the guys back. Drill Dickens kicked a guy down in his trench.

"Don't you fucking get up!" Drill Thompson ordered.

"Don't any of you get the fuck up! Hold the perimeter! Next person to leave their post is getting their ass recycled back to week one!"

The tornado sat in the middle of the field before it started moving away from us. The wind died down the further it got away.

I couldn't believe how close it got; scared the piss out of me. As I kept my eyes on the field I imagined what could have happened if it had come toward us. Not much we could have done except brace ourselves and hope for the best.

I learned an important lesson that day: no matter how big of a shit storm, I needed to follow my orders and fight through it. Drill Dickens told us a weak soldier could put a whole squad in danger. Stay strong in any storm that comes your way, no matter what you feel inside.

*   *   *

After graduation from basic and medical training, I received orders to Ft. Hood, Texas, where I was assigned to Echo Company, a medical unit in the 15th Forward Support Battalion with the 1st Cavalry Division. We provided support to the mechanized infantry units within the division. I was informed the day I arrived that we'd be flying out to Iraq in three months. From then on, all we did was train for the worst.

I was assigned to the ambulatory platoon. My main job would be evacuating patients from the battlefield. We trained for weeks out in the field, evacuating patients in our ambulances and M113 armored medical tracks (we called them tracks for short; they're like mini-tanks with metal tracks instead of wheels). By the time January came around, I was sick of training and ready to go to war. All I thought about was being stuck in a desert for a year fighting; couldn't help but think that it was meant to be. The reason I joined was to fight for my country; I just wasn't ready to die.

*   *   *

Bang! Bang! Bang!
"Get up! Everyone up and out, we have formation in 40 minutes! Gotta go, gotta go!"

"Shit!" I sat up in bed and checked my watch, "Shit, I overslept. Marc! We're gonna be late," I called out, peeking my head over the dresser to see that he was still asleep.

I jumped out of bed, threw on my desert camouflage uniform and grabbed my hygiene bag. On my way out of the room I kicked his bed as hard as I could.

"Wake up Marc! You're gonna be late to ship out. First sergeant's gonna have your ass."

He started tossing and moaning as I closed the door, stumbling down the hallway to the bathroom. I still felt drunk, the taste of alcohol fresh on my breath. The first thing I did was brush my teeth.

Hans came barging through the door with matted blonde hair, smelling worse than me. He looked around the room,

"Boney?"

"What's up man?" I said.

"You seen Jacob? I can't find him anywhere." He slowly made his way to the sink.

"No, I haven't seen him since last night."

"Dude, I think I'm still wasted," he said, staring into the mirror rubbing his eyes.

"Fuck, me too. We drank a shit ton. I need something to eat," I said with a grin.

"I've gotta take a shit," he laughed, then turned to the stalls, trying to open the closed door.

"Who is in the stall?"

"I don't know; they've been in there since I came in."

Hans knocked on the door.

"Hey who's in there? I've gotta take a shit," he yelled.

He kept knocking "Hey hurry up...you ok in there?"

Someone started moving around, their belt buckle jingling while they struggled to get their pants up. The toilet flushed and out walked Jacob, a short Latino guy, shirtless, holding up his pants.

"What the fuck time is it?" he said with a heavy Spanish accent, guarding his eyes from the light. Hans and I started laughing.

"It's morning man." I said. "We're about to ship out to war."

Jacob held his stomach "What the fuck. All I remember is using the bathroom. The next thing I know you fuckers are banging on the door."

"You've been in there all night?" Hans asked laughing. Jacob nodded with a moan. We laughed even harder.

Sergeant Till opened the door, startling us.

"Hey, get a move on before you're late; everyone else is downstairs getting their weapons."

"Yes Sergeant!"

I ran back into my room and tore the blanket and sheets off my bed, stuffing my personal belongings in my duffle. It was an awkward feeling knowing this was the last time I'd wake up in America. I didn't know if my upset stomach was nerves or a killer hangover. I tried not to think about it as I rushed downstairs with my gear.

Green duffle bags, protective vests and helmets were neatly stacked in rows on the grass. I stacked my stuff in formation then ran inside our company CP.

"Boney's here, Top!" said Sergeant Till as I came through the door. Everyone was standing around chatting.

"Go sign your weapon out and wait for formation."

"Yes Sergeant."

I walked over to the arms room and waited in line behind Specialist Scott, a short and stocky southern boy. He started sniffing the air and turned around. "God you reek man." He chuckled, "Smells like someone had a blast celebrating."

"Wasn't that much fun, couldn't leave base because no one had a ride. We just drank and listened to music. What did you do?"

"Spent time with my wife."

"Oh yeah, she's due pretty soon, huh?" I said.

"Yeah, another month or so. Hope they let me take leave to see her."

"Sign here." Specialist Ray held up the clipboard.

Scott grabbed his rifle and signed for it. I did the same and followed him outside. My squad leader, Sergeant Robbins was standing off in the shadows of the building, smoking a cigarette and drinking coffee. He's as tall as me but a lot thinner; I could always tell who he was by how he hunched over with a cigarette.

"You got a smoke?" I asked walking up to him.

"Don't you got your own yet?" he said, opening his box of Marlboro's. He tossed one to me; I caught it mid-flight.

"You know I don't normally smoke. I just need one to wake me up. Can I use your lighter?"

"Want to borrow my lung too? Geez." He said sarcastically, tossing me a lighter.

"I'm still drunk from last night man, give me a break."

"Told you guys not to drink a lot. I told you."

"I told yah," I said, mocking him in the most girlish voice I could. "At least I enjoyed myself before going off to war."

"Yeah, me too. I just didn't go overboard." He pointed over to the barracks, "Those two are way late." Jacob and Hans were falling over themselves trying to get their stuff downstairs.

"Jacob fell asleep on the toilet last night." I started laughing quietly, trying not to draw any attention.

"Oh yeah?" Robbins chuckled too. "I'm going to give him so much shit." He bent over, putting his smoke out on the cement. "Happy birthday, by the way," he said as he headed over to the CP.

"What's so happy about it?" I asked taking another drag. He laughed on his way inside.

Just my luck, twenty-first birthday and I'm flying off to war. I wasn't legally allowed to drink until today, but I've been legal enough to kill for three years. Didn't make any sense. I'll have my next drink a year from now, if I make it.

Sergeant Hill yelled for formation. I ditched the smoke and ran over. First Sergeant Tanner (Top) walked out of the CP and stood in front of formation along with the commander.

"Company!" he yelled out, "Attention!"

We snapped to attention and yelled our company name, "Echo!"

Chapter 7: North Victory

It was badly storming out by the time we got to the base. Rain was pouring on us as lightning tore through the sky. After the long convoy, I was ready to get my feet planted somewhere. We rolled up to the main entrance; the walls of the base stretched as far as I could see, with watchtowers posted every 100 yards or so.

The guards at the gate had rain pounding off their ponchos, their faces stone cold angry when we passed by. I figured it wasn't pleasant having to pull guard all day out in this shit, sitting in the freezing rain, hoping no one attacks.

We passed row after row of large green tents lined up right off the road as we made our way through base. I saw the 3rd I.D. patch posted up outside of a building on a wooden billboard. Soldiers dressed in their desert camo uniforms (DCU's) were walking alongside the tents, watching our convoy go by.

At the other end of the base, we came to a section with rows of small white trailers. Our convoy came to a stop in an open patch of sand behind the trailers.

"This is it," Sergeant Robbins said; "our home for the next year."

"Great, home sweet home."

We got out of our vehicles when we saw Top walking down the line. He ordered us to meet Specialist Ray at the new CP to get assigned bunkmates and trailers so we could secure our gear and set up operations.

Halfway there I saw Specialist Reynolds rushing toward me, "Yo! Boney," he yelled as he quickly walked past me, slapping my shoulder, "you're with me bro!"

Reynolds is a kid from Jersey with a heavy accent. If I was to room with anyone for a year it was going to be him. We had each other's backs; I trusted him.

"Seriously?" I asked, trying to keep up with him.

"Yup, there's perks to being in supply." He tossed me a key. "Here's your key, come on let's go find the trailer."

We walked down rows of the trailers until we found ours, a hundred yards from the outer wall. There were two twin beds and a dresser inside. I was excited that we didn't have to sleep on cots for the next year. I tossed my medic pack inside.

"Man I'm glad I got you as a roommate," I said. "Fuck, everyone else except for Hans has problems."

"Yeah it would be a different story if we could be co-ed though." Reynolds said, humping the air and slapping an imaginary ass, "I'd be with Briana, beating it up all day like, uh-ah-huh."

"Oh yeah, how is that going?" I asked.

"Yeah, I'm gonna have those drawers by the end of the week," he said grinning.

"We'll see," I said, "Fucking lucky. Twelve months out here; I'm gonna need to find someone." We laughed.

"Go find you some pussy man. Run up on a chick, grab her ass and be like "Wanna fuck." Reynolds joked.

"Ha! Funny, if it were only that easy."

"Bro, Sergeant Brown's got her eye on you. I see how she be battin' those eyes when you come around. I can hook you up, bro," he said, holding out his hand.

"Eh, I'll pass for now."

Reynolds started laughing. "Yeah ok, let me know after a couple months of this shit hole."

Someone knocked on the door.

"Who is it?" We both yelled.

A woman's voice hollered, "Sergeant Hill!" I quickly opened the door.

"Boney," she said in a high-pitched voice. "Get out here and start helping us set up these tents."

"Yes, Sergeant Hill. Just getting my room straight." She looked over at Reynolds.

"Reynolds, what are you doing?" she demandingly asked. "You can help too."

Reynolds' eyes darted back and forth, "Sergeant, I've gotta go over to the CP and help out Top," he quickly said.

"Ok," she said giving him an evil look, "I'll ask him when I get over there. You better be telling me the truth."

"Hooah Sergeant! I am," he said with a smile.

"Boney, let's go!"

It took us two hours to get the medical tent up. The rain made the sand muddy. It was difficult to walk around; my boots would sink into the ground forcing me to struggle to keep them on my feet. My pants and boots were covered in thick mud by the time we finished; I was exhausted.

Reynolds, Top, and our company commander, Captain Nero, came walking in the tent. "Attention!" we yelled.

"Carry on," Captain Nero said. He started walking around inspecting the tent.

"Well it looks good," he said, stopping in front of us. "We have the generator coming over as we speak."

"The brigade commander will be coming over to welcome us." First Sergeant said, "We have formation in..." he looked down at his watch ... "10 minutes out here in the motor pool."

"Hooah Sergeant."

"Let's actually walk over there now to be a little early," he ordered us.

"Yes First Sergeant."

We all walked outside and gathered over by the vehicles. The whole battalion was out there; flag bearers from the companies were standing in the front of formation, flags swaying in the air. We started hearing loud bangs in the distance. The ground shook after each one. The sound of gunfire echoed in the distance as Command Sergeant Major (CSM) Davenport brought the battalion to attention.

"Gamblers!" We shouted out.

CSM Davenport handed us off to the general.

"Alright Gamblers! Welcome to North Victory. This will be your home for a while, so get comfortable."

While he was talking the fighting in the background grew louder; the ground shook more violently. I couldn't hear what the general was saying between the explosions and the weapons fire; all I could see were his lips moving.

A stream of dirt and smoke suddenly gushed out from the ground next to the platoon across from us. Within seconds a second round screamed through the air and planted in the ground next to Ray and me.

My heart jumped as I felt the ground shake through my legs; a fuzzy numbness grew in my chest. Smoke crept into the air out of the ground; all

I could do was stare at it. People were looking over at us. I wanted to say something; maybe even run, but the general was here and no one else did anything so I just kept calm and looked up front.

He stopped talking and brought the battalion to attention, "Right step march!" He ordered, Left..." He maneuvered the battalion around the hole.

"Battalion, Halt."

He ordered someone to mark the spot where the mortar had landed and then finished talking to us. The weapons fire died down in the background.

I tried listening to the general; staring at him wide eyed, but I couldn't concentrate. A mortar just landed right next to me and didn't go off. Shit, I couldn't believe that just happened. I silently thanked God that it didn't go off; imagining what would have happened if it did. I could be in a body bag on the way home.

After he ordered us out of formation, Ray turned around slowly; the color was drained from her face. I could tell she was in shock.

"You ok Ray?" I asked, but all she did was stare at me looking void of any life; I felt the same way inside.

*   *   *

It was dark by the time I was relieved from guard tower duty. I had spent the last two weeks watching rocks and deserted homes. The only people I ever saw were kids. They'd run up to us and beg for water and candy.

"Water Mista?"

"No!" I'd yell down, "No water for you, get the fuck back."

"Candy?"

"No. Get back." Adults were usually squatting in the background as if they had sent the kids up to ask. Our orders were no talking to anyone, not even kids. I heard stories of insurgents using them as distractions for bombs and mortar attacks. I didn't want to fuck up, so I was never nice. They usually stomped away upset.

My stomach was growling by the time I was dropped off at headquarters. I walked over to Sergeant Robbins' trailer to ask if he wanted to grab chow. When he didn't answer I walked the mile stretch down the road towards the DEFAC. I decided to stop inside the company trailer to see if anyone wanted to eat.

Reynolds was sitting behind a desk next to a green military radio inspecting his weapon. He was on 24-hour duty with Sergeant Flynn. We each had shifts listening to the radios for medical evacuations.

"Wanna go grab some chow?" I asked Reynolds.

"Fuck yeah, I'm starving. Hey sergeant, can I take my break?"

"Sure," he said. "I'll go when you two get back."

"Thanks Sergeant." He got up and grabbed his gear.

We walked across the gravel road to the DEFAC. It was set up in a group of connected trailers. After we ate we went back to the company trailer and Sergeant Robbins was laughing with Flynn.

"Where were you Sarge?" I asked. "I was looking for you to grab chow. I knocked on your door."

"I just got off duty from the aid-station."

"Ah, never thought to look there," I said.

Gunfire started echoing through the air, followed by a loud thud and an explosion right outside the trailer. We fell down flat to the floor.

"What the fuck is that?" I yelled.

"Aw shit! We're getting fucking attacked!" Reynolds screamed. I watched as he slapped a magazine in his rifle and cocked it back, loading the chamber; I did the same.

"What the fuck do we do?" he yelled as he crawled across the ground over to the window.

"Shit!" I yelled seeing a bright flash and a loud explosion. A heavy exchange of weapons fire filled the air.

"I'll call it in!" screamed Sergeant Flynn.

I could hear him calling the battalion HQ as the firing seemed to fade away.

"It stopped," Reynolds said, staring out the window.

"What the fuck were those explosions?" I said, "They were fucking close."

"Fuck yeah they were," Reynolds said, still panting, holding his weapon tight.

I heard yelling all around us from outside. Then we heard a call from the HQ asking for medical evacuation at Tower 16. I had just gotten off duty at Tower 17, not even an hour ago. Sergeant Flynn dispatched an ambulance from the aid-station. A couple minutes later I heard Sergeant Martin's voice over the radio, "We have a male with multiple gunshots en route."

I sat there and thought about being up in the tower getting in a firefight; *what if it was me who got shot?* It could happen tomorrow; another eleven hours until my next shift. My stomach turned at the thought of it.

Sergeant Flynn radioed for a Medivac; the chopper flew directly over us en route to the aid station.

"OK men." Sergeant Robbins said sarcastically. "We're all safe now thanks to you. You can stand down and clear your weapons."

"It's not funny, Sarge," Reynolds said. "We could all be dead right now, shit."

"Yeah I know big man, I know." Robbins and Flynn started laughing.

We both cleared our rifles and went outside to smoke a cigarette. After a while Sergeant Martin and Jacob walked up to us with blank looks on their faces. They told us it was Sergeant Dotson; he got hit three times in the chest. He was stabilized before they evacuated him.

I knew Sergeant Dotson well; he was a mechanic in our motor pool. I had talked to him a couple times to get work orders done for my vehicle; in fact, I just saw him yesterday. It was easy to be killed in war. It could happen to anyone at any time.

The next morning on my way to the DEFAC with Sergeant Robbins, we saw Private Watson sitting outside his trailer with a scrub brush and a bucket of water. He was scrubbing the blood out of Sergeant Dotson's protective vest. I could see holes through the front on the chest area. Tears were running down his face.

"You doing alright?" Sergeant Robbins asked. "What happened?"

"I'm getting Dotson's gear and personal belongings together to send home," he mumbled.

"Have you heard how he's doing?" I asked.

"He almost didn't make it," he said. "He's stable in the green zone."

I was glad to hear he made it. We both told him it would be ok and headed off to breakfast. The only thing going through my head that day was it could be me; maybe next time it would be me.

Chapter 8: Death and Disorder

I woke up to the sound of praying over a loud speaker. It was too early; I hated listening to it every morning, not being able to understand a word they were saying. After it stopped I tried falling back to sleep. My stomach started growling, so I jumped out of bed frustrated and threw my gear on.

I walked over to Sergeant Robbins' trailer and knocked on the door; knocking again harder after I didn't hear him answer.

"What?" he yelped.

"Come on Robbins, let's eat. I'm starving."

"Alright, I'm getting up."

I lit up a smoke while I waited for him. It always took him a long time to get up. He walked out of the trailer lighting up a smoke.

"Ok, let's go."

After eating chow we walked to the motor pool to get our ambulance. It was basically a Humvee with a box on the back to hold patients on litters. The doors weren't even armored; we had to weld thick steel plates on the doors when we first got to base. I swear we had the crappiest vehicles in the division. Every other unit I saw had armored vehicles.

I walked to the back of the vehicle and picked up the rubber block from behind the wheel, unlocked the door in the back, and threw the block in. Sergeant Robbins climbed into the passenger seat and turned on the radio. He called the aid-station to let them know we were on the way over. I climbed into the driver's seat and drove onto the gravel road towards the aid-station.

We parked outside the tent and started helping the platoon load patient litters onto the back of a large truck. When we were done loading, we got in formation and waited.

Top brought us to attention and took head count. Captain Nero came to the front of formation and briefed us on our mission for the night. First Cavalry was conducting a 400-house raid in search of weapons and insurgents. We were to provide aid to any casualties during the mission.

When we were released from formation, we took a convoy to Camp Slayer. The lead vehicle took us to a large brick building near the edge of camp to set up operations. Sergeant Leo and I parked our vehicle right next to a wall around the corner. We got out and started setting up the emergency room in an open bay. Litters on litter stands with saline on poles were at the ready for immediate vein access.

Sergeant Hill gave us a briefing on how we were operating that night – who was working where. The mission commenced at 1500 hours. I was assigned to the triage group, to help the nurse intake patients then help out where I was needed. If there were any casualties, they had to be assessed by triage then taken to their designated areas for care. Medics were to be at their assigned stations until the end of the mission.

Sergeant Robbins and I went to eat chow right after getting released. We ate quickly so we could catch a nap in the back of our ambulance before the mission started. We climbed in and took off our gear. Robbins took the top litter leaving me on the bottom. I was tired and it was hot; I knocked out in no time.

Boom! I woke up startled with the vehicle shaking. It felt like someone had bumped into us. I got pissed thinking I should open the doors and check it out. Sergeant Robbins was snoring right above me so I couldn't hear much outside.

"Sergeant Robbins?" He kept snoring away.

Boom! The whole vehicle shook.

"Sergeant Robbins!"

"What, wa-," he said groggy.

"Did you feel that? I think we're getting bombed."

"I didn't hear anything," he said, sounding annoyed. "Go back to sleep…"

A louder blast shook the vehicle harder. I jumped out of my litter and opened the back doors. As soon as I cracked it a mortar hit the ground right outside sending dirt and smoke in the air.

Shit!

"Fuck Robbins, we have to go." My heart was beating fast as I put my helmet on and grabbed my vest. He wasn't getting up fast enough, "Now!"

We both had our gear on half assed as we hopped out of the back and ran over to the bunker. Mortars pounded down even faster; the ground shook as I ran. They hit buildings and landed on the ground with explosions that rattled my body and made a piercing ring in my ears. At one point I knew I'd be hit but I kept running, telling myself I wanted to live. The gray-cement boxed shelter was only 60 yards away. I hoped one wouldn't hit me; imagining what it would feel like if it did.

We jumped inside the bunker with a couple people stooped over, waiting patiently inside with stiff faces. A Major was sitting on a worn down crate, hunched over, slowly smoking a cigarette. He didn't look as afraid as we were; I didn't understand why. The rounds came in for another couple of minutes before it got eerily quiet.

We sat inside the bunker listening, thinking there might be more coming in. The only thing I heard were people screaming and crying in the distance, "Medic! Medic!"

Sergeant Robbins and I feverishly ran over to the aid-station. Injured soldiers were limping in from all over being assisted by other troops. Some were walking over on their own, holding their own bloodied limb.

I ran over to the first person I saw. It was a woman. She had specks of shrapnel up the right side of her face, oozing blood. I helped her over to the triage area and handed her off to Sergeant Hill; she was waiting with a medic pack.

The engine of a truck pulling up behind me made me turn back around. A deuce and a half truck was backing up towards us; people were laid out in the back. I heard a girl screaming and crying so I ran over. "Help…someone help him, Ahhh!"

"Here!" I yelled, stopping at the back to open the door. "I need the most injured first."

I yelled over towards the aid-station. "I need help over here! Hands!"

A soldier dragged someone on a litter to the edge of the truck; I helped take him off the back. The guy complained the patient was too heavy; we ended up setting him on the ground.

The casualty had a blood-soaked bandage tied around the top of his head. Part of his scalp had been sliced open; I could see the crack in his head open and close as he had small convulsions. I reached down and tried to hold him still. I placed a hand on his scalp trying to hold the bandage on.

"Can you see me?" I asked, staring at his eyes to see if he was responsive; they were faded, light blue, and glazed over. I'd never seen anything like it; they were void of any life. There was blood seeping out from the bandages; someone did a poor job wrapping it.

Sergeant Hill and a couple soldiers came up from behind me. "I'll grab his head Boney, help carry him in." I let go of his head as she reached in. On the count of three we lifted him up and ran him into the aid-station. Sergeant Hill was on the side of us holding the top of his head like his life depended on it. I knew he wasn't going to make it but that didn't mean we wouldn't do the best we could to save him.

We got over to the litter stands and set him down. As soon as we let go the trauma team and doctors rushed in and took over. My gloves were full of blood so I trashed them then started to look around to see if anyone needed my help. I didn't see any new patients so I ran over to where Sergeant Robbins was.

"Boney, I need your help loading patients."

"Roger Sarge. Who are we getting first?" I asked.

We went inside and grabbed a soldier who took a mortar to the leg, but didn't go off. Instead, it broke his shin so it was bent at a ninety-degree angle. He was praying the whole time we carried him; a couple of his buddies were holding his hands praying too. We put him in the back of the ambulance then ran back in and loaded a girl who took shrapnel to the arm; it sliced through her brachial artery so she had a tourniquet. Every time I looked at her she looked as though she was going to pass out. The color was drained from her face; blood splatter covered the left side of her body. We closed up the back of the ambulance and I gave Sergeant Martin the go ahead; they took off with two gun trucks headed for the green zone in downtown Bagdad. As I watched them leave the gate a Blackhawk flew over me.

"Let's go see if they need help," Sergeant Robbins said.

As soon as we got in, the doctors yelled for hands. I ran over to the guy with the head wound; he was wrapped in new white bandages with tubes coming out from his chest. We lifted him up and rushed to put him in the back of our ambulance. Sergeant Robbins and I drove him over to the helipad with Jacob and Hans in the back to help.

There was a Blackhawk with a big red cross on the side, the medic standing outside patiently waiting. We ran him over to the helipad, ducking down as we passed under the thumping propellers throwing gusts of wind down. As soon as we got him in we ran away and watched as it took off flying low just above the buildings.

Sergeant Robbins and I took out our smokes, lit'em up and started puffing away. We didn't talk at first; we just stared at each other trying to comprehend what just happened. The mission hadn't even started yet and we took casualties. My mind drifted back to all the injuries and blood; the engulfing feeling of chaos and death. I should have been injured or dead by now. Every mortar that hits close to me is a dud; I must be lucky. I wish everyone were as lucky as me.

I looked at Robbins, "What the fuck bro? That was fucked up." He looked at me with a pale face.

"Yeah...it was; good job, by the way," he uttered before taking another huge drag from his smoke.

"Thanks."

When we finished our smokes we drove back to the aid-station to help with clean up. I couldn't stop thinking about the casualties, each one running through my mind over and over again.

After we finished, the whole company sat around the aid-station. Sergeant Hill thought it would be a good idea to talk about what happened. Most of us sat silent; the only thing I could say was "That was fucked up."

We learned the guy with the head wound had died on the way to the green zone, minutes after he left. He was twenty-two years old and just got into the country yesterday. One day in and he died. It was hard to comprehend. We sat around the aid-station talking about death the rest of the day. Robbins and a couple guys started talking about the way we wanted to die.

"If I go, I hope it's painless," I said. "I'd take a mortar to the head; at least I would be out of it until I go."

"I'll take a bullet to the head," Robbins said.

"Fuck that, I hope it's a bomb," Jacob piped in. "Then there would be no way I'd feel a thing." We all agreed with him.

Chapter 9: Twenty-four Hours

I shot straight up in bed, panting heavily, drenched in sweat. One minute mortars are blowing up all around me, the next I'm waking up surrounded by darkness gasping for air. It always took a moment to realize I was dreaming and didn't die; it felt surreal.

Our A/C wasn't working; the heat made it harder to stay asleep. Our generator broke two days ago. I guess it blew because of the God-forsaken heat. It had been over 130 degrees the whole week. We'd been without power ever since. I'd spent the past few nights smoking a hookah outside with all the guys, waiting for it to cool down enough to fall asleep; it usually did around midnight.

I walked over to Sergeant Robbins' trailer and knocked on the door.

"Get up Robbins!" I cried out when he didn't answer, "We have to go eat before our shift."

Sergeant Flynn opened the door. Robbins was in bed with his blanket pulled over his head.

"Hey, Boney."

"What's up Sergeant Flynn? Robbins told me last night to wake him up; we've got 48-hour duty at the aid-station."

"I'm up. I'm up." Robbins sat up, swinging his feet off the bed. "I need a coffee and a smoke," he grumbled.

I grabbed my pack of smokes and shoved one in his face.

"Ewe, I wouldn't smoke a Newport unless I had to." He grabbed his from his pocket.

"Picky, picky Sarge," I said. "A smoke's a smoke in my opinion. I'll smoke anything."

"Don't you know Newports can kill yah?" he asked with a bit of sarcasm.

"Fuck, I thought all smokes kill you," I said smiling. "Have to die someday."

We ate breakfast then I walked down to the motor pool to start inspecting our vehicle while Leo went to the CP to sign it out. Halfway through my inspection I heard one loud gunshot; it sounded close.

"What the fuck?" I looked around wondering where it came from. It was weird to hear only one; especially inside the base. I figured someone went to clear their weapon and a round was left in the chamber. *What a dumbass,* I thought as I went back to my inspection.

A minute later Sergeant Robbins came running towards me with a cup of coffee splashing around in his hand.

"Boney!" he cried. "Boney turn the radio on. Someone got shot, we gotta go now!" He hopped in the passenger side as I flipped the radio on and started the engine.

"Yeah we got her. Headed to the aid station," I heard Sergeant Wake say over the speaker.

"Oh fuck. Ok the other ambulance got her." Robbins said as he sipped his coffee. "Phew. I'm relieved. Did you get done with the checklist?" he asked me.

"Yup. Want to go early and check out what happened?" I asked.

He looked at his watch. "Sure, I guess we can relieve them early."

I drove down to the aid station and parked in the back. We hopped out and went inside. A team of people was surrounding a girl on a litter. There were tubes coming out of her chest along with an esophageal tube sticking out her mouth. There were blood soaked bandages covering her chest.

"Did you call for that chopper?" one of the docs screamed out.

"Yes sir, I called six minutes ago," Jacob called out from the corner of the room. He was sitting down listening to the radio.

At that moment I heard the thumping of a Blackhawk as it flew over; the tent swayed violently from the air currant.

"Ok finished!" Doctor Rose yelled. "Let's go! Grab her and go! Move!" He backed away holding his hands up, soaked in blood. Sergeant Robbins and I helped load her onto the chopper.

"What a way to start a shift," Robbins said as we watched the chopper take off.

"Yeah, crazy," I said, "How did it happen?

"She shot herself with her rifle," Sergeant Wake said in her southern accent, walking up behind us with a smile on her face. I was surprised.

"Fucking determination! All to go home, it isn't worth it."

"Hell no," said Sergeant Wake. "If I go home it's gonna be from actually getting shot or blown up. Shit, I couldn't kill myself; I love me too much."

"She's just a coward," Robbins blurted out. "Sorry, if I offended you, Sergeant Wake," he said, holding out his hand chuckling.

"None taken, asshole." She rolled her eyes. "Anyway, so… you guys going to let us go early?"

"Yeah, yeah go on get out of here." Robbins said waving her away, "We can take over."

"Ok, thank you gentlemen," she said, happily walking away. "Hope your shift is better than ours. Ciao!"

We parked our vehicle and went inside to help with morning sick call. I helped take soldiers info and vital signs while the doctors did the exam and diagnoses. Ill Iraqi people from the villages outside the gate came through once in a while. The two main diagnoses were dehydration and the flu.

After our lunch break we drove Captain Rose and an interpreter to the detention camp on base to do medical rounds. We parked our vehicle outside the fence and waited to be escorted through the complex. We passed by a couple prisoner trailers on the way. The prisoners were dirty and dressed in rags; one was pacing back and forth; others were squatting down, staring while we walked by. I noticed they didn't have air conditioning units like ours; guess that was a luxury only we had.

Walking into the main building I saw two small cells. In one, a man was sitting on a bed, rocking back and forth moaning. Another man was sitting on the floor in the other cell murmuring things at us. I could hardly understand a word he was saying. The only words I could were, "Mister" and "water please."

A guard walked over and told him to shut up. We walked past and were brought into a common area with showers and tables.

We set our packs on the picnic table in the middle of the room and waited. Minutes later a guard escorted the first prisoner into the room. He looked beat up and drained. I couldn't tell whether he was sweating or if he was soaked with water; he smelled like he hadn't taken a shower in years with his dirty blue rags on. The guard sat him on the bench and chained his wrists to the steel legs.

We started checking his vitals; I took his blood pressure while Captain Rose looked him over. He grabbed a light and told him to open his mouth. The translator spoke and the prisoner slowly opened his mouth. His tongue was bleeding, but I couldn't tell from where.

"What happened here?" Captain Rose asked the prisoner. He muttered something pointing to the guard.

"They did it," said the translator.

The guard turned, "Lying little shit." He looked at the captain; "He keeps fucking biting his tongue, doc. Trying to act like we did something to him. He just wants special treatment."

The prisoner shook his head and pointed at the guard, talking fast to the interpreter.

"He said that they did it. He says they hit him and make him bleed." The guard gave him a cold look.

Captain Rose sighed then checked his tongue,

"Well, it looks superficial. He'll be ok."

The next guy they brought in was quiet. He sat down on the bench not saying a word while we checked his vitals. He was dehydrated; Captain Rose suggested he drink more fluids and watched as he drank a quart of water.

Rose started talking to one of the guards about how they treated the prisoners. He said, "It is ridiculous to always see the prisoners dehydrated or bruised up."

It was true; every time we came here the prisoners had something to complain about. I had a feeling something was going on; but there was nothing I could do about it; they did something to get detained. None of them were innocent. For all I know these guys could have helped plan the mortar attack yesterday; why else would they be in here? Why should I care? We're at war with these people. As long as they don't kill them with chains on, I'm Ok. I would expect to get my head chopped off if they captured me; they are the lucky ones.

After our last patient we packed up and drove back to the aid-station. The rest of the day went by slowly. Around 2100 hours Sergeant Robbins told me I could catch some shuteye while he stayed in the aid-station. I climbed into the back of the ambulance and quickly fell asleep, only to be awakened by the back doors jerking open.

"We have an incoming from an IED." It was Sergeant Robbins. "Get ready."

I hopped out the back and ran inside the aid-station to hear what was going on. Someone was yelling over the radio, "We just rolled through the main gate." He was panting hard, "Stay with us man! Stay with us."

Sergeant Robbins and I ran out to the dirt road. Headlights of the incoming vehicle were beaming through the air as it came winding around the road, heading our way. They sped around a corner and came to a grinding halt next to us.

We ran to the back of the Humvee and anxiously opened the doors. Two troops hopped out, the casualty was screaming and moaning. I helped pull him out on a litter. Blood was everywhere in the back of the vehicle; his legs were a shredded mess. He had tourniquets on both thighs. We rushed him inside the tent and placed him on the stands.

The trauma team swarmed at him and quickly went to work. I turned back towards the door to see two limp bodies being carried in; blood dripping over the floor. The soldiers carrying them were crying. They started screaming profanity, "Those fucking savages, fuck man! Why? Why?"

We asked them to leave so the doctors could work better, and called for a Medivac as the doctors worked to stop the bleeding.

"What's the ETA on the chopper?" Captain Rose yelled. As if on cue, we heard the chopper coming in overhead.

"It's here!" I yelled.

"Ok, let's get this patient out!" Captain Rose shouted backing away from him.

I ran over and helped lift him up and out of the tent. We ran to the helipad and loaded him inside. The other casualties were being placed into body bags as we walked back into the tent. We called the HQ for escorts to transport the bodies to the green zone. That was the main reason we were here on duty. Ninety percent of the time we drove to the green zone was to transport bodies.

We loaded the bags into the ambulance and waited an hour for the escorts. I was always nervous to convoy at night, especially after seeing what could happen. A bomb could be anywhere along the road. We wouldn't see it until it was too late. My heart raced as we hauled ass down the freeway to the green zone, hoping we didn't blow up.

Chapter 10: Days/Nights

"Yo!" Reynolds yelled, yanking open our trailer door. Sunbeams came pouring in, forcing me to squint my eyes open.

"Can't you be quiet, man? I'm finally getting some sleep," I said groggily as he walked to his bed.

"Man, I'm trying to hop in these showers while they're working."

That surprised me. "The showers are working?"

"Yup. I'm gonna be one of the first ones in there. It's gonna be nice and hot!" he said excitedly.

"Well fuck, I might as well get up and take one too. I'm fucking dirty." I hopped out of bed.

"I don't need you in there to hold my dick bro; girls like it when you smell." He smiled pushing me back on my bed.

"Fucking dipshit. Get the fuck on." I kicked at him, narrowly missing as he ran out the door laughing.

The shower was freezing cold. It felt like the water was bouncing off the dirt film stuck on my body. I've used bottled water and baby wipes to wash up for the past two weeks; it would have been nice to have hot water. I jumped in and washed as fast as I could, and ran back to my trailer. As I opened the door something exploded, knocking my hearing out and shaking the ground. It sounded like a mortar hit.

Sirens blared all around. I slammed my door and sprinted over to a cement bunker two trailers down. Specialist Frey was already under the bunker; I sat down across from her and waved. She waved and went back to staring at the ground.

I was used to mortar attacks. Once you get in the bunker it's about riding it out. It used to be a painful experience looking around with a 'What the fuck do I do' look on my face; jumping with every explosion. Now I stared into space, hoping that one didn't land on top of us.

I looked at Specialist Frey; she looked at me. I stared at the wall knowing she was thinking the same thing; *I want to be home.*

Suddenly it went silent. My ears rang as my hearing slowly came back into focus. The silence was cut by screams, "Medic!"

I immediately ran out of the bunker yelling to Specialist Frey, "I'll grab my bag! Call it in!" I ran to my trailer, threw my pack on and rushed over towards the screaming. Two rows over I saw smoke rising in the air as the smell of burning rubber hit me. I turned the corner. Specialist Frey was kneeling next to a soldier, radioing for an ambulance. Two other soldiers were sitting on the ground holding their arms.

I ran over to Frey and opened my pack, "I got this one, take care of the other two." She grabbed bandages and gloves out of the bag and ran over to them. I asked the girl questions about her injuries while putting on gloves. All she did was cry about how bad her leg felt.

I tore open her pant leg and saw shrapnel up and down her leg. There was a big hole halfway up her thigh badly bleeding out. I broke open an aid-bandage and held pressure on the wound to stop the bleeding. Ten to fifteen minutes of pressure is certain to stop any bleeding other than arterial, (medic 101).

Brakes screeched next to me as an ambulance pulled up. Sergeant Martin and Specialist Dole hopped out. I told them to bring a litter over to me.

I finished tying the aid-bandage as they ran up to me. We rolled her onto the litter and strapped her down and placed her into the back of the vehicle. The other two climbed in with Sergeant Martin and I closed the doors. They shot down the road toward the aid station.

I snatched my gloves off, walked over to the trashcan and threw them away. Specialist Frey helped me pick up.

"Alright, I guess I'll see you later." I said.

She smiled, "Bye. See you at formation."

When I turned around I saw a guy standing in front of a trailer; the only one that was hit. He was staring at the huge nine-foot hole in the side of it.

"You ok man?" I asked, wondering what he was doing.

"Yeah," he said, "This is my trailer. I left one minute before the attack, to use the bathroom."

I became entranced with the hole; my head was full of 'What-ifs?' Like what if my trailer was hit when I walked in? It was only 30 yards away. I figured that's how this guy was feeling. People walked over, snapping pictures with their phones.

I ran back to my trailer and rushed to get dressed, hoping I could hurry down to the aid station to help out. When I arrived, the two troops with the arm injuries were bandaged up, waiting to be released. They had called a chopper to evacuate the leg wound. I spoke to Hans about what happened. We joked around about the ways we could have died, trying to make light of the situation. Deep within my heart I was scared though. I just never showed it; there was no room for fear. With every mortar that hit, my heart felt stuck in my throat, but I always swallowed that fear when I had to jump into action thinking my life isn't as important as saving someone else's.

The rest of the day was spent sleeping and talking about the hole to whoever asked. Sergeant Hill told me I did a great job with the response; she said I might even get an award for it. I didn't really care. The only thing that mattered to me was if the girl survived or not. The whole scenario kept cycling through my mind whenever I was alone. I thought about how I could be better; what I needed to improve on for the next time. There was always a next time.

*   *   *

I was running relentlessly through the desert, sweating and panting, filled with fear. Mortars exploded all around, engulfing me in vivid bright colors. The ground shook as if the world was falling apart. A sinking sensation grew inside my chest. I felt like my heart was being pulled through my body, beating faster, growing heavier as it fell away. I struggled to breathe as ear-curdling screams surrounded me.

My body burned at the sight of blood pouring in; the image of a decapitated soldier lingered in front of me. My eyes locked onto his; they faded from green to a glazed light blue as I watch his life slowly drain away. The world spun around; my body was being pulled into a million different directions. I struggled to breathe as the ground shook. Closing my eyes, I tried screaming as I fell into a dark hole, but nothing came out. Suddenly I shot up in bed panting, not knowing where I was.

An explosion made me jump; seconds later my trailer shook. It didn't take me long to realize it was just a dream. I crawled out of bed and lit a smoke to calm my nerves. As I opened my door another explosion went off. A yellowish-orange dome filled the sky over a trailer in the distance for a second. It was the artillery.

A white-hot streak shot through the sky; flying out into the darkness. While looking at the light, a shock wave hit; my legs shook as the ground rumbled from the explosion. A white haze lit the night sky when the round hit; a minute later I'd hear a faint explosion. They shot a round off every two to three minutes.

I imagined what it would be like on the other side. It had to be ten times worse than a mortar attack; bet it shredded every building and person within range. I hoped they were hitting their targets dead on; I'd seen too many casualties for us not to win this fight.

Chapter 11: The Mission

I was startled awake by a knock on my door. I stayed quiet hoping they would go away but they knocked again.

"Who is it?"

"Sergeant Brown!"

I rolled out of bed and opened the door.

"What's up Sergeant?"

"Boney. I need you up and ready within the hour. Pack your duffle for at least a month; we're going on a mission."

I was stunned; it was the middle of the night.

"A mission? Where are we going?" I asked.

"I don't know the details right now but we have a briefing in 30 minutes. When you're ready meet me at the CP. Make sure your aid bag is topped off; if you need something, make a list and I'll get it for you."

"Roger, Sergeant," I said, closing the door as she walked away.

I looked at my watch; it was two in the morning. I got excited and nervous at the same time, not knowing what to think. It had to be a pretty important mission to be up in the middle of the night. It felt like a training exercise back in basic.

I got dressed and quickly packed my gear. My aid bag was good so I grabbed my rifle and headed out the door. It was dark and quiet out; the row of trailers seemed deserted. There was one trailer door open, with a yellow light beaming out. As I got close, Specialist Saul walked out and started dumping water out of his canteen. He was the only one in our company with a bald head and mustache.

"Yo, Saul!" I yelped, approaching the door.

"What's up Boney?"

"What you up for? You going on this mission too?"

"Yup. Do you know what it's about?" he asked.

"Nope. Sergeant Brown just woke me up and told me to get packed for a month."

"Same here," he grinned, "must be some shit if they're getting us up this early."

"My guess too." I looked at my watch. "We should head over to the CP. Briefing's in 10."

He locked up his trailer and we walked over to the CP. We heard a bunch of commotion when we walked in. Top and Lieutenants Hobbs and March were talking to each other around the front desk. Sergeant Brown was sitting on the couch in the corner looking over some paperwork.

"Here Sergeant," I said walking up to her.

"Good, right on time. Why don't you guys go check out night specs for the mission, we'll be heading out soon for the brief."

Immediately after we checked them out Top brought us over to the briefing room. It was packed with troops from the other companies. The battalion first sergeants and commanders were sitting at a large oval table in the middle with the enlisted soldiers standing around.

A few minutes later the battalion command sergeant major (CSM) and the commander walked in.

"Attention!" the room stood up to position,

"At ease," the commander said, sitting down at the middle of the table.

"Ok gentlemen," the commander said, "I guess you're all wondering what we're doing here tonight." He grabbed a remote and turned on the projector, a picture of a city popped up on the white board.

"The 1-5 and 2-7 Cavalries have been activated to support operations in An Najaf. In the last three days the Mahdi army has taken control of the city and are held up in the Imam Ali Shrine; the third holiest in the world. Marines have been unsuccessful at combating them and as always they need us to come in and save their ass."

We all laughed quietly.

"Ok, Ok settle down. I asked for the best troops we have for this mission; that's why you are all here. Our mission will be to support the infantry units as they fight off the insurgents until we take back the city. The mission will not end until that is achieved, Roger?"

"Hooah!" we all cried at once.

"That's what I like to hear," he grinned.

*   *   *

We were standing in pitch black next to our vehicles when Lieutenant Hobbs walked up to me, "You ready for this, Boney?"

"Oh yeah, Lieutenant, I'm ready. Shouldn't be that bad right?" I said hopefully.

135

"Huh, I think it will," he said with a stern look.

"The marines haven't been able to fight them off, that's something," he said. "It's pretty bad out there; I heard they're making IED's out of barrels and rolling them down the street at our men. You sure you're ready for that?"

"Hooah sir. I'll be all right… I'm ready," I said uncertainly. Deep down I was nervous. "Whatever comes my way, I can handle it."

"You nervous?" he asked grinning,

"Yeah, just a little bit. Nothing I can't handle though."

"You'll be alright big man! Stay safe out there. Make us look good, Hooah."

"Hooah sir!"

"You get a chance to call anyone, tell'em where you're going. You won't be able to talk to anyone for a while," he said.

"No sir, I don't have a phone."

He pulled out a cell from his pocket, "I'll let you use mine if you're quick."

"Cool Lieutenant. Thanks." I grabbed the phone.

"Remember this mission is top secret, so you can't tell anyone what we're doing. Just let them know you love them."

"Ok." I walked over to our ambulance and dialed my dad's number.

He answered groggily, "Hello?"

I spoke quietly, "Hey Dad! Did I wake you up?"

"Yeah. It's Ok though, what's up? How's it going?"

"It's going good. I can't talk to you for long though, I just needed to call you to tell you that I'm going on a mission and I don't know when I'll be able to talk to you again."

"What? A mission?" he said surprisingly, "What kind of mission, where are you going?" he sounded just as nervous as I was.

"I can't tell you that, sorry. I just wanted to call you and tell you I love you."

"I love you too man. You doing something dangerous?" he said nervously.

"I don't know, maybe. Can you make sure you tell everyone I love them if something happens? Make sure you call grandma and ask her to pray for me."

"Oh damn…," he sighed. "Sure I will, you know that. Sam, stay safe. Be careful."

"Ok Dad, I'll try." I heard everyone yell for formation in the distance. "Oh, I have to go, Dad. I love you."

"I love you too man. Talk to you later."

"Bye Dad." I hung up feeling like that was the last time I was going to talk to him. In my heart I knew something was going to happen, I just didn't know what.

I tossed Lieutenant Hobbs his phone as I ran into formation; giving him a thumbs up that I reached someone. CSM Davenport walked to the front of formation and shouted, "Group attention!"

"Gamblers!"

*   *   *

We got inside our ambulance in the middle of a fourteen-vehicle convoy made up of fuel tankers, tow trucks, and mechanic work trucks. After a quick radio check, we took off out the front gate.

We moved fast, screeching around corners as we made our way through town. After passing Abu

Grab prison, the lead vehicle made a left turn onto the ramp for the highway. As soon as the second vehicle made the turn, white and red bullets lit up the sky from buildings all around. Rounds bounced off the sides of vehicles and ricocheted off the concrete ground. My heart sank as I heard rounds hitting our vehicle; nervous that someone would get hit.

The convoy sped up; vehicles in front of us kept turning onto the ramp. I hoped that we wouldn't run into any bombs in the road, my nerves were on edge as I steered the vehicle.

I looked over at Sergeant Brown as I turned onto the ramp; she was crouched down below her weapon with the barrel pointed out the window.

"What the fuck are you doing Sarge!?! Fucking shoot'em!" I screamed at her. "Shoot at something!" I knew she was my sergeant but I didn't care. The way she cowered, not saying a word made me more angry.

I turned and hit the gas hard. We sped down the ramp as bullets ricocheted off the front of the vehicle. My heart was pumping; I was furious she wasn't shooting. She should be the one driving; I couldn't believe it.

We made it onto the freeway out of the line of fire. The tanker in front of us had something dragging behind it shooting up sparks from the road. I kept my distance so it wouldn't fly back and hit us. After a few miles we took an exit off the freeway to do damage assessment.

I kept snapping at Sergeant Brown, "What the fuck is wrong with you? You didn't fire one shot!"

"I didn... I didn't see anyone," she said, stuttering.

"You should have fucking shot at the fucking muzzle flare in the windows! Haven't you ever heard of suppressive fire?"

"Sh-shut up Boney!" she shot back at me.

"I'm your sergeant! Don't tell me what to do. I'll write you up if you don't shut up now!"

I closed my mouth, trying not to say anything. When we stopped I snatched my rifle and jumped out. I walked around the vehicle to see if there were any damages.

"Whoa," I heard Saul say as I walked back to the front. Saul and Sergeant Brown were staring at windshield on the passenger side. The windshield was cracked; shaped like a spider web. A round had hit it right where Sergeant Brown's head should have been. It was creepy. I could tell she was shocked because she couldn't take her eyes off it.

Chapter 12: The Convoy

We arrived in camp Anaconda just before sunset. The convoy leader said we were staying for a while; the roads ahead of us were getting ambushed most of the day. We parked next to a brick wall on the perimeter and were told to grab chow and meet back at the vehicles for further instructions.

On our way back mortars started raining in, exploding everywhere. I got worried when I realized I didn't know where the bunkers were. I darted my head back and forth looking for one. Sergeant Brown pointed to some troops going in a building so we followed. Dozens of rounds landed already and they kept pouring in.

Eight other people were cramped in the bunker when we reached it. Explosions rocked us from all around, shaking dust from the barricade's ceiling. The minutes dragged past before they stopped.

On instinct I listened for screaming; I heard someone, but it was far away. I asked Sergeant Brown if we should go help, but she told me we needed to get back to our vehicles to check in; there would be someone to help.

The lieutenant was holding formation in front of the vehicles patiently waiting for everyone. After he checked our names off, we stood in line at ease to wait for everyone. Troops trickled back; after 5 minutes everyone was accounted for.

The lieutenant let us know we'd be staying until they figured out a safer route. We all got assigned tents and bunked down for the night.

*   *   *

At daybreak we were back in our vehicles, hauling ass down the freeway. We stayed on the same road for miles, seeing nothing but camels, sheepherders, rocks, and sand passing by. I needed a distraction to keep me awake. The hum of the engine, along with the heat, was working against me. Sergeant Brown was nodding off; she wasn't any help. Saul stuck his head through the middle door every now and then to talk, but most of the time I had to put my headphones in. I blared

Greenday and Jay-Z to keep myself awake. It was the only way to stop myself from falling asleep.

If I was in my civilian clothes in a topless corvette, I might be enjoying this trip right now. I put down my window and let the wind blow over my face into my hair and looked over at Sergeant Brown with a fat smile. She rolled her eyes then pointed to the road. Saul reached over and tapped my shoulder. I took my headphones out.

"Could you not jerk the vehicle so I can go number 2?"

"Ah man, fuck. I don't want to smell your shit." I shook my head, "Yeah I'll try."

We rarely stopped on convoys, which forced us to think up crafty ways of relieving ourselves. It was hard taking a piss or dump in a moving vehicle. I usually saved a water bottle to piss in then tossed it out.

Saul stuck his head out again, "Can I use your MRE bag? You don't need it, right?"

"Nah bro. Go ahead I'm good."

"Thanks." He closed the doors. A few minutes later he opened them back up and I was hit in the nose with foul shit.

"Oh, dude, you reek," Sergeant Brown cried out.

"Can you throw it out your window for me Sarge?" he asked with a grin, passing the bag to her.

"Fuck no; you do it. AND DON'T GET ANY ON ME!"

She put down her window. I laughed as Saul slowly reached over her and tossed it out; Brown gagged like she was going to barf. I couldn't stop laughing.

We got to the outskirts of a city when the lieutenant's voice came blaring through the radio, "Ok, eyes open; be on the lookout for anything suspicious. Reports say this town is usually a hot zone, but we need to get through. It's a perfect place for an ambush."

One by one each vehicle checked in, "Trauma one, Roger that."

The road took us straight to the middle of the city. We were going at a good pace before we hit a crowd of people. We honked our horns moving slowly through the streets. Suddenly the convoy pulled over and we came to a halt.

"Ok team," the lieutenant said, "we just had someone run up to our vehicle talking about a box underneath the bridge ahead. They think it's a bomb. Everyone get out and be on guard while we check this out."

The city was crowded; there were people moving about everywhere. We were next to a bazaar; people were stopping at different shops along the road. Some walked by, staring at us hard through the shawls over their heads; others walked past minding their business. Men were standing in the distance with AK's slung over their shoulders. It felt like the enemy could pounce on us from anywhere. I gripped my weapon tight with my finger on the trigger ready to eliminate any threat.

Kids lined the roads shouting, "America. America." And begged for candy and water, "Candy Mista…Water?"

It was too noisy. I felt vulnerable not being able to see what everyone was doing, what they were holding. If something went down, a lot of us could get hurt. I kept my eyes open, darting my head back and forth, carefully watching. We stood there for what seemed like a half hour before the Explosive

Ordnance Disposal Specialists (EOD) came speeding past me driving a large beige boxed vehicle. They drove to the front of the convoy.

Ten minutes after, I saw a huge puff of smoke go up from underneath the bridge. A loud rumble with a gust of wind rushed past me; the shockwave felt like I was going to be knocked off my feet. Everything went silent as my ears rang. It took a while to hear the city again.

The lieutenant hopped back on the radio "Ok, we are going to move back out. Keep your eyes open."

EOD flew back past us as we moved out. When we drove past the bridge I saw a huge crater in the ground where the bomb was. It had a black ring around it, still smoking. I was happy to know that it had been found; I thanked God for the warning.

This was the second close call we had on the convoy. I got nervous as I started thinking about how much worse it might get. My mind kept flashing back to all the IED casualties that came through the aid station; the mangled bodies and decapitations. A chill ran down my spine as we drove out of the city and into the desert.

*   *   *

We rolled up to Camp Duke through a small, deserted town. There were marines out on the front gate and in watchtowers along the walls. Lieutenant drove us over to the motor pool where our vehicles would stay.

We immediately reported to the 1-5 Cavalry Medical Platoon Leader, Staff Sergeant Bricks. He quickly put us to work setting up the aid-station. We made two triage stations; emergency patients would be taken inside a brick building where the doctors worked. A tent was set up outside for treating minor wounds. Staff Sergeant Bricks let us go for chow when we were finished.

Halfway through dinner, shells started hitting base. Sirens went off as we ran and got under the bunkers outside the DEFAC. We heard a bunch of gunfire exchange before the sirens and explosions faded off. We didn't hear anyone yell for a medic, so we walked back into the DEFAC and emptied our trays. On the way out we heard screaming. A couple of troops ran by with a guy on a litter wrapped in bloody white bandages. He was screaming in pain.

"Aaaugh, Ahhhh Fuck!"

The soldiers shouted at everyone to get out of their way as they ran to the aid station. I wanted to help out in some way so I ran after them. When I got to the aid station, enough soldiers were running around helping with treatment, so I stood back. If I jumped in it would do more harm than good. They were treating three casualties; two hit with shrapnel and a guy with his leg blown off. There was a group of soldiers watching in the doorway crying. I could tell they were in his squad. You only cry for people you care about.

A few minutes later a Blackhawk landed on the helipad. Soldiers ran out with the amputee and loaded him in. We helped with clean up as soon as the other two patients were treated. There was blood all over the ground. It took an hour of scrubbing to clean it all up.

*   *   *

Right before nightfall, Staff Sergeant Bricks gathered all of us in formation to give us an in-depth briefing on the mission. He stood in front of the platoon with a map of Najaf on a whiteboard beside him.

"At ease," he shouted. We held our hands behind our backs.

"Now then, operation kicks off at 0600 hours." He pointed to a red circle on the map, "This is the Imam Ali Mosque, third holiest shrine in the world. As you know the Mahdi army is holed up inside and has taken control of the city. We will be in joint operations with the marines, 2-7 Cavalry, and 227 aviation units to fight the enemy and take back control of the city."

"This is the Wadi-us-Salaam cemetery," he pointed to a large area within a yellow circle, "a 7-mile stretch surrounding the city. Most of our fight will be here. Our forces will box them in on all sides and push them back into the city.

"Our mission is to assist with the operation, and take care of the casualties as they come in. This will be a tough fight. Command says this will be the first hand-to-hand combat the United States has seen since Vietnam. Any questions?" No one raised their hands; everyone stood quietly.

"Good. Now everyone will be on field rotation. If you are needed on the front lines you will be thrown out. So make sure your rifle is prepped and ready. Hooah!"

"Hooah," I shouted along with the group.

On the line? I thought. *Shit.* I didn't expect that. My chest burned as my thoughts raced. Every casualty I helped flashed through my mind. I didn't want to end up like them.

After we fell out of formation Sergeant Brown walked up to me, "You have first radio watch with me tonight."

"Roger that Sarge. Can we really be thrown on the front lines?"

"Yes. You worried?"

"No," I said quickly, "I just never expected my first fight to be in a cemetery," I said, surprised.

"I don't think we'll be needed, it'll be fine. Let's report in."

The radio was quiet all night. A Specialist Hunter came looking for Sergeant Brown the next morning while she was at breakfast. I talked to him a while before she came back. Seemed like a nice guy; he said they'd been friends for years.

When I got back from chow they were sitting close, laughing and smiling. I could tell they had a thing for each other. She blushed every time he made her laugh; I thought it was weird, seeing that she was married. I wondered how friendly they were.

Chapter 13: Casualties

We had had fifteen casualties since the start of the mission, three with life-threatening injuries; and troops keep dropping. They say the front line is hell on earth. Fighting in a cemetery filled with dead bodies, with temperatures above 140 degrees, I could see why.

We sat idle in an empty lot with two gun trucks just outside the kill zone. I heard explosions and weapons fire echoing through the air while sitting in darkness in the back of the ambulance. All I did the whole time was hope and pray no one would get seriously hurt.

A few hours into the shift a call came blaring over the radio for an evacuation. We immediately shot out of the lot with the escorts, heading straight into the battle. A couple sharp turns and the gunfire got louder. I heard multiple explosions close by, moments before we came to a quick stop.

"NOW!" the driver yelled.

I forced open the back doors, dropped the stairs and jumped out. Soldiers were crouched behind a crumbled wall next to us, firing into the graveyard.

Four troops came rushing towards me; one was turned firing off shots as he ran. A guy with a scruffy beard had blood spewed all over the front of his shirt holding an aid bandage on his hand. I helped him into the vehicle and jumped in. A couple seconds later we were speeding off towards base.

"Those fucking...F-Fuck!" the sergeant screamed, throwing his weapon to the ground. "Lousy fucking sons of bitches!"

"Come on Sergeant, sit down," I said. "Let me check you out."

He gave me a cold stare then sat down on a litter, sticking his hand out towards me. I unwrapped the bandage; the tip of his right pointer finger was blown off. Blood was running out so I pressed it back on his finger. The bandage was full of dirt and soaked with blood so I decided to rewrap it.

"Damn, what the fuck happened out there, Sarge?" I asked, reaching over to grab a new aid bandage.

"We were chasing a fucking towel head that shot a rocket at us." He started panting hard.

"We chased him into a parking lot when we came under heavy fire. I took lead in advancing when some fucker jumped out from behind some rubble and shot my trigger finger."

"Fuck. Did they at least get him?"

"That ass hole dropped a second later, fuckin' bastard."

I switched out bandages quickly then held pressure on his finger.

"Ah!" he yelped

"Sorry Sarge but you have to hold it tight to stop the bleeding, ok?" I said.

"Sure Doc."

"He got what he deserved… fucking bastard. I can't believe he hit your trigger finger."

"We got his ass though, that's all that matters," he said grinning.

"Hooah. Glad you're safe, Sarge."

"Thanks, Doc."

When we got to base I handed him off to the aid-station; then we drove back out to the empty lot and sat on standby.

*   *   *

I was chatting with Saul in the back of our ambulance in the middle of the afternoon when we heard shouting over at the aid station. I looked around the back doors to see soldiers running around; Sergeant Bricks was shouting orders. Saul and I grabbed our rifles and sprinted over to see what the commotion was.

I ran up to Sergeant Brown when I got to the tent, "What's up Sarge?"

"We have incoming, three guys seriously wounded."

"What should I do?" I anxiously asked.

"Help out where you can."

We stood around the radio quietly listening to the chatter. After a couple minutes we heard the driver say he was rolling through the front gate. I looked over to see a huge cloud of dust rapidly shooting through the air behind the wall. It swerved through the base as it made its way towards us.

A swarm of people with cameras was standing by the unloading area; I figured they were reporters but I didn't have a clue why they were waiting.

That's when Sergeant Bricks called me and a couple other guys over to him.

"I want y'all to go over there and hold those reporters off; we've got patients to take care of. I don't want them vultures getting in the way taking pictures. Do whatever you need to without hurting them, understood?"

"Hooah Sergeant!"

We all ran over and stood in a line in front of them. They eagerly fiddled with their cameras, taking practice shots at us while they waited. As soon as the Bradley came bolting around the corner towards us they started taking pictures. I was curious as to why it was a Bradley and not one of our medical vehicles they were taking pictures of. Bradleys were primarily used as armored heavy assault vehicles like tanks. They were used to transport infantry units into battle, not out.

"Hold hands!" I heard Sergeant Bricks yell, "Don't let anyone fucking through!"

The Bradley came to a screeching halt behind us, covering everyone in a cloud of dust. The reporters rushed us. We held each other's hands as tight as we could against the onslaught; I looked to see someone open the back hatch and lift out the first casualty. The reporters came at us hard, pushing and shoving, flashing their cameras non-stop.

We were screaming at them, "Get the fuck back! Fucking move!" It wasn't working. I could barely hold on to the people next to me.

Through all the chaos, a reporter broke through and rushed to the back of the Bradley, rapidly flashing pictures. One of the sergeants stood tall then tackled him hard to the ground; his camera flew up and landed in the sand. We moved back as Sergeant Bricks helped push him back outside the line.

The first casualty was covered in dark red blood; his arms fell limp off the side of the litter as the medics ran him into the operating room where the docs were waiting. The reporters kept shouting at us, "You can't do this. We have rights!" while they took what seemed like hundreds of pictures.

Sergeant Bricks was right; they acted like vultures. The first site of blood and they jumped at it like it was their last meal. I couldn't believe they wanted to take pictures of someone's kid like this;

just to get on the front page. My stomach turned, thinking about them collecting a check off of a soldier's death.

The second casualty was covered in blood too; they ran him over to the tent. A soldier crawled out the back of the Bradley in tears. He started swearing and kicking the sand.

"Fuck…fuck. I couldn't do anything. I couldn't." He broke down falling to his knees covering his face with both hands. A couple medics tried calming him down; they got on the ground and held him as he cried. It was the only thing we could do; his wounds were far too deep for us to help. He just went through hell and lost his closest friends.

A couple guys were struggling with the last casualty. "We need hands!"

I rushed over and helped lift him out.

"He's gone!" I heard one of the soldiers say with tears running down his face.

We ran him over to the aid station, but Sergeant Bricks redirected us to our sleeping quarters. As soon as we walked through the door the chaos seemed to vanish; the flashing lights and screams went faint as we walked into the dimly lit room. We set him on the floor two feet away from my cot.

I got a good look at his injury as we set him down. A hole the size of a golf ball was blown through his chin. The back of his head was blown out; dark red blood dripped through the litter onto the floor. For some reason I couldn't stop looking at him. The guys with me stared too.

One of the docs walked in with Sergeant Bricks, he pronounced the soldier dead and started filling out his paper work. Sergeant Bricks handed me a body bag.

"Ok, soldier," he said, "we need to bag him up and clean up this mess. Have a couple guys help you."

We put gloves on and slowly placed him into the bag, then loaded him into the back of an ambulance for transport. My body felt numb, my stomach queasy, as I tried my hardest to think of something other than the dead troops, as we cleaned up. My gloves stayed covered in blood; they were always covered in blood when shit like this happened. It always left me with the dreadful feeling that one day it would be my blood.

When I left to get more cleaning materials, I saw soldiers standing outside the operating room crying as they watched the doctors work. I was walking back in the building when I heard someone scream. I looked to see medics walking out with another troop in a body bag.

A Blackhawk flew over the building a second later. Medics ran out of the room with the last casualty wrapped in white bandages with tubes coming out everywhere. As soon as they got him on, it took off. I heard people asking the doctors if he would make it when they stepped out of the operating room. All the color had been drained from their faces as they shook their heads.

A medic explained to us what happened. The squad was in the cemetery taking a break in the back of their Bradley when an insurgent jumped on top and opened fire into the turret, shooting everyone inside. The only reason that one soldier survived was because his buddy fell on top of him when he got shot, saving him from the ricocheting bullets.

*   *   *

Later that night, Saul, Brown, and I were asked to help a reporter out with anything they needed. We helped them unload their camera equipment and set it up outside of a building. They said they needed extra hands to help hold the big antenna while they did the live broadcast to CNN. I didn't have patience for reporters after the stunt they pulled with those troops, but I was ordered to help. Plus, I was hoping I might be able to get on TV to say hi to my family.

The reporter opened up a computer as Saul and I held the antennae. A few moments later two windows popped up on the screen, one with the camera room director and the other was the live broadcast from the station. I saw Solidad O'Brian chatting with another reporter. After talking to the director, the reporter jumped in front of the camera and made some adjustments.

They gave the reporter a countdown; then he started talking. It was cool seeing how this stuff was done. While listening to the reporter I thought about how many people I knew that could be watching this. I bet everyone at home knew about the hell we were going through right now.

Reporter: We are seeing a gruesome fight taking place here in the battle of Najaf. The U.S. marines and 1st Cavalry are fighting the Mahdi Army through the streets of the city and the Wadi-us-Salaam cemetery. The enemies are using catacombs underneath the cemetery to attack and evade our troops. Some people are saying this is the first hand-to-hand combat the US has seen since Vietnam. The Mahdi army is also held up in the Imam Ali Mosque, the third holiest shrine in the world, making it an even harder fight for our troops because they simply cannot fight them in there for diplomatic reasons. Our soldiers are relentlessly fighting day and night in what seems like a never-ending battle. Both sides have sustained heavy casualties, but the fighting has not let up.

Chapter 14: The Front Line

I was walking back from brushing my teeth in the morning when Sergeant Bricks and Sergeant Brown came running up to me.

"Boney!" Sergeant Bricks barked. "You need to get your gear and report to the aid-station; you're needed on the line."

He threw me off. I stood at ease thinking I was dreaming. Sergeant Brown butted in…

"Sergeant, Sergeant!" She was yelling beside him trying to get his attention.

"Yes, Sergeant Brown?"

"I want to go out, send me instead! I'm his sergeant; I have more training than him. I'm supposed to go out!"

I looked at her crazy; what the fuck did she think she was doing? I didn't need her to make me look weak.

"At ease Sergeant!" he yelled in her face. "You know full well we won't let women on the front line. What will America say to a woman being killed in battle, Huh?"

She stared through him with a distant look as he kept screaming, "The only reason he is going is because you can't. Boney, hurry up and grab your shit. They're on their way to get you."

"Hooah Sergeant!"

I ran back to my cot and got my equipment on. I was shocked. My mind kept flashing back to the troops who died yesterday. The gaping hole dripping out blood – that could just as easily have been me. I haven't lived a full life yet; this was the first time I ever thought about it.

Every person I've seen injured flashed through my mind. I didn't want to end up like any of them. *"Shit!"* I said to myself, snapping my chinstrap and throwing on my medic pack.

"Boney!" Sergeant Bricks yelled through the open door, the sunlight blinding me, "You ready?"

"Roger Sergeant, moving out!" I snatched my rifle and ran out the door. *I bet everyone's a little scared before going out. Maybe this is normal; I can do this.* My thoughts raced as my chest burned while waiting next to the aid station.

"You good?" Sergeant Brown asked as she ran up to me.

"Yeah Sarge, I'm good," I said.

"Boney, they just drove through the main gate," Sergeant Bricks yelled to me.

"Hooah Sergeant!"

"Good luck out there. I know you'll do good; you're a fine medic," he said.

"Thanks Sergeant." When the ambulance pulled up I jumped in the back and we took off.

I sat in silence with blue light shining on me from the corner. As we drove I heard people on the outside; crowds yelling and shouting at us in Arabic, a lot different from the America chants I was so used to hearing. We moved slow trying to pass through. A couple rounds pinged off the side of the vehicle; good thing it was armored.

After making a couple turns we came to a stop; it sounded like multiple gunfights were only yards away. We sat a moment before the passenger got out and opened the back doors.

When I jumped out I saw we were next to a medic track. We were in a fenced parking area across from what looked like small broken down carnival rides. The cemetery was directly across the street; there were tombs as far as I could see.

The back of the track dropped down and a thin, rough looking old sergeant walked out.

The sergeant I was with started talking, "Sergeant Yates, this is Private Boney, the replacement."

"Private." He nodded at me, I nodded back.

"You can jump in the back."

"Hoo-ah Sergeant." I walked over to the track and climbed in. I took my bag off and set it in the corner.

"Yo, how's it going?" I said to the driver.

"Hey," he said with a wave then went back to concentrating on the radio chatter.

Sergeant Yates spoke to the other sergeant for a while before walking back in the track.

"Close'er up!" he barked at the driver; the back lifted up and slammed shut.

"Private Boney, this is Private Bailey," Yates said. Bailey waved again, "How's it going?"

"Eh-I'm here," I said; they both chuckled.

"Yeah, I hear you," Bailey said.

"Well, welcome to the team Private," Yates said. "Try to make yourself comfortable; we'll be here for a while. Keep an eye out for the enemy; they like to pop up every now and then."

"Roger Sergeant."

I popped the top of the track open and stood up to look around. It was hot; even though we were in the shade it was still 135 degrees. Most of the time we sat listening to radio chatter of the fighting going on across from us. Bailey liked to crack jokes every now and then but Sergeant Yates wasn't much of a talker. He just sat in the turret chewing his dip and laughing at the comments we made to each other. We grew quiet whenever we heard gunfire and explosions, on edge waiting to hear if someone got injured.

A couple hours into the shift we felt the ground shake from an explosion, then a heavy exchange of gunfire ensued. Someone came over the radio, "Team three to base, we need a Medi-vac now!"

Bailey fired up the engines as Sergeant Yates radioed back, "Roger that team three. En route." I closed the top hatch as Bailey gunned it.

We took off down the street toward the fight. I sat down bracing myself as Bailey turned corners and drove down the bumpy roads. Gunfire echoed louder outside the track as we rolled into the heat of battle.

Sergeant Yates started firing his pistol, swearing out loud, "Fucking bastards! Shit!" I heard bullets zip through the air and bounce off the side of our vehicle.

Bailey stopped and yelled at me as he dropped the hatch, "Ok, let's grab him!" I stepped out with my weapon raised, ready to give suppressive fire. Rounds ripped past me as I saw three guys running over to me; one of them was limping.

When they got to me I grabbed the soldier and helped him onto one of the litters in the back. His team threw his weapon and his gear on the ground then ran back out to the fight, shooting frantically downrange, making their way to cover.

Bailey lifted the hatch and took off. The soldier had shrapnel up and down the right side of his body. He already had an aid bandage on his leg and his head. I checked him head to toe to see if he was bleeding anywhere else, adding a bandage to his arm when I saw blood trickling from a hole.

When we got to the exchange point the hatch dropped open. Saul and another medic came in to assist with loading him on the back of their ambulance.

"How is it out there?" Saul asked.

"Crazy shit man. Rounds flying everywhere." It was all I could say before he closed the doors and took off towards base.

Sergeant Yates said I did a good job as we drove back to the empty lot. We joked about how close the rounds came to hitting us. After a couple hours a convoy of Bradleys and M-1 Abrams tanks rolled down the street in front of us toward the cemetery. It was the 2-7 Cavalry coming to replace us.

After they switched out with the teams, we got into a convoy and headed back towards base. We went through the same crowd of screaming people; this time they were throwing things at our vehicle. When we got back to base Sergeant Yates ordered me to get some rest and to meet him back at the track in the morning for the next shift.

When I got to my sleeping quarters I took my gear off then ran over to the latrine hoping to take a shit and shower. When I got there the door was locked with a sign posted, 'NO WATER'. It didn't surprise me though; it was always when I desperately wanted to feel clean that nothing worked. I still needed to use the bathroom so I walked to a Port-a-potty. I was hit in the face with an overwhelming smell of crap when I opened the door; it hadn't been emptied in days because of attacks. Waste was piled up to the top of the seat. It was fucking disgusting; I'd shit on the ground outside if I wouldn't get in trouble for it. Needing to go badly, I squatted Indian style above the seat and went. I hate living like this. The only thing I wished for was to kill every insurgent in the city and to get a shower and a clean shitter.

*   *   *

After breakfast, I reported to Sergeant Yates in the motor pool.

"Boney! You get enough sleep? Ready to go?" Sergeant Yates asked.

"Hoo-ah Sergeant; as much sleep as I could."

"Alright, good. Hop in the back; we roll out in 10."

After radio check, we rolled out the front gate back to the cemetery. On the way out the commander was on the radio singing the marine song, making fun of them,

"They always need us to save their ass!" he shouted. Then he played the 1-5 theme song, "Who Let the Dogs Out? Who, who, who, who."

We took our place in the lot when we arrived at the cemetery. The 2-7 Cavalry waved at us as they rolled past looking happy to get the fuck out of here. I would be too; the heat was relentless during the day. It was 115 degrees already and the sun just came up. I drank water and Gatorade like crazy, only to sweat it out minutes later.

We went most of the day without casualties. It was towards the end of the shift when we got a call over the radio for a Medi-vac. On our way in we learned it was a medic that got hit. As usual we rolled under heavy fire; I felt multiple explosions rock our vehicle.

Three soldiers came running over when the hatch dropped; I jumped out and helped the injured soldier on. As soon as the hatch was up we raced down the road out of the kill zone. The soldier was mad; sweat poured down his face as he swore out loud.

"Fucking marines! I fucking hate'em."

"Whoa, whoa, calm down bro. I've gotta take a look at you. What happened out there?"

"Lousy fucks!" he said, panting hard, "I was up on a sniper position about to take someone out when I heard something land next to my hip."

"I looked over and saw a grenade, I had just enough time to scream and roll off the building; the blast caught me as I was falling off the roof. We fucking saw it was one of those marine bastards before we started getting attacked."

I took off his vest and opened his shirt; he had three small holes bleeding out from his left shoulder. I tore open an aid bandage and held it tight against his shoulder.

"You hurt anywhere else bro?" I asked.

"Naw, man," he replied.

"Can you breathe Ok?"

"Yeah, I'm good."

I wrapped the bandage around his shoulder.

"I think you'll be alright man. Just some shallow pieces. Make sure you hold this tight to stop the bleeding."

"Yeah, Ok. I hate marines," he said with a moan. I could tell he was fuming inside.

I helped him into the ambulance when we got to the extraction point. When I sat back in the track we bolted back down the street.

"Boney!?" Sergeant Yates shouted.

"What's up Sergeant?"

"We're bringing you back to the line to join his squad."

My heart leaped into my throat and started beating hard. *Oh man!* I thought, *Fuck.* I got nervous.

"Roger Sergeant."

"Get your gear ready; we'll be there in three."

"Hoo-ah"

I threw my bag on and strapped it tight. All the injured troops I've seen from this battle started flashing through my mind. The blood, the lost limbs, and the guy I placed in a body bag with the blown out skull; I couldn't help it. I gripped my weapon tight and stared at the wall. My chest burned; I felt like hurling, but instead took a couple of deep breaths. My mind was racing; *my first time on the line; in a cemetery?*

A thousand reasons went through my head on why I shouldn't be there; I was too young, I didn't want to die. But then somewhere within the cloud of fear a thought hit me; this is what I've been trained to do. Only cowards fear death and I wasn't a coward. All of sudden I knew this was it. It was my moment to shine whether I got shot or not; no turning back now. I forced myself to think positive, *you can do this, you can do this.* I couldn't have fear out on the line, that's how people die. Remembering the storm back in basic; the promise I made to myself not to panic; I swallowed my fear.

A prayer came to mind that every medic learns in training, the Combat Medic prayer. It was the only thing I could think of to calm myself down. I raced through it in my head over and over again:

Oh Lord, I ask for the divine strength

To meet the demands of my profession.

Help me to be the finest medic,

Both technically and tactically.

If I am called to the battlefield,

Give me the courage to conserve our

Fighting forces by providing medical

Care to all who are in need.

If I am called to a mission of peace,

Give me the strength to lead by caring for

Those who need my assistance.

Finally, Lord help me take care

Of my own spiritual, physical

And emotional needs.

Teach me to trust in your

Presence and never-failing love.

AMEN

"Get ready!" Sergeant Yates yelled to me. I heard heavy gunfire as we pulled up to the battlefield. The back hatch dropped open.

"Good luck!" Sergeant Yates told me as I walked out the back.

"Thanks Sergeant!"

We were right next to a Bradley with its hatch down; a soldier was waving me over to him. I ran over and hopped in the back.

"Boney?" a lieutenant asked.

"Yes sir!"

"I'm Lieutenant Jackson!" He shook my hand. "Sit tight; we need to wait for the team to be safe before you go out there."

"Yes sir!"

I sat and listened to the exchange of gunfire and explosions as the fight went on. The team radioed for assistance as mortars started landing. The Bradley moved in and out of the cemetery firing shots at enemy. There was a screen in the back where I could see whatever the cannon was pointed at. It was infrared; everything that gave off heat was a bright white, the structures around were grey and black.

The camera came into focus on someone shooting from behind a building. He stood up and fired a couple rounds, then crouched back down behind the wall. I listened to the gears shift as the Bradley moved into position setting the cross hairs on the body, then lit him up.

The blast from the cannon was extremely loud; I didn't expect it. I covered my eardrums as they throbbed and rang. The white body shattered into pieces as the rounds hit him. I never saw anything like it before; it looked like a video, only I knew it was real.

Minutes later the lieutenant radioed the team to pull back and load up, the replacements were there.

The hatch dropped open as the squad ran into the back. They were panting, looking tired and worn as they yelled at each other about the gunfight they just went through. I sat back and listened, feeling out of place. After a while everyone calmed down. The sergeant introduced himself and the team.

"What's your name soldier?" he said.

"Boney, Private Boney."

He reached over and shook my hand, "Good to have you with us. My name's Sergeant Hunter, the squad leader." He pointed over to the other guys, "That's Specialist Bates, B for short. He's Private Martinez, and that's Rodriguez."

"What's up guys," I nodded to them.

"Yo! 'Sup," they greeted me, sounding exhausted.

"Welcome to the team, soldier," Sergeant Hunter said, then laid back and closed his eyes.

Chapter 15: Ghosts in Hell

I could tell everyone was pumped when I woke up. Specialist Baits, a tall country boy, was pacing the tent mumbling under his breath; he looked like he was in his own world. Private Martinez was sitting on his cot, checking his radio equipment. I cleaned my weapon while we waited for Sergeant Hunter and Specialist Rodriguez to come back from a briefing.

Rodriquez, a slim Latino guy, poked his head through the tent, "Let's roll out boys." I grabbed my medic pack and walked out the tent with the other guys.

"It's hotter than a whore in church out here," Sergeant Hunter joked; we all chuckled.

"Ok, guys. It's going to be over 145 out today; another day in hell as usual. Mission is the same, nothing's changed. Boney?"

"Yes Sergeant?"

"How much fighting have you done on the line?"

"Um, none Sergeant. Just the training we went through when we came in the country."

"Ok. Well, you're going to get a lot of experience today." The guys chuckled. "I'm going to teach you some things as we go. Make sure you keep up; it'll be fast paced. Hooah?'

"Hooah Sergeant."

We walked over to the Bradley. Lieutenant Jackson and Private Young were already there, getting ready. Sergeant Hunter told me to load up with as much ammo as I could hold. I grabbed four extra magazines, filled them, and stuffed them in my left cargo pocket.

Sergeant Hunter told Martinez to give me as many grenades as I could hold. He threw me one. It had duct tape wrapped around, holding the clip down with pin pulled out.

"Grab as many of them as you can hold and prep them just like that."

I prepped five more and stuffed them in my cargo pocket. I handed the pins to Hunter; he put them up in case we didn't use them all.

"Let me see your rifle." I handed it to him. After he inspected it he gave it to Rodriguez and grabbed his M16 with a M203 grenade launcher attached.

"Your primary job, when shit hits the fan, is to lay down heavy suppressive fire. You know how to use the grenade launcher?" He held up Rodriguez's weapon.

"Yes Sergeant, learned in basic."

"Good." He tossed it to me. "Grab as many rounds as you can." I grabbed four hi-explosive rounds and stuck them in my grenade pouch and medic bag. When I thought about all the grenades I was carrying I got nervous. All it would take was one round to hit a grenade and blow me to bits.

"Don't get nervous bro," Rodriguez said. It must have been written all over my face. "With as much fire power as we have, they're the ones that need to be nervous." He laughed.

"I'm good man, thanks," I said, trying to throw a poker face on.

The lieutenant ran past us up into the Bradley. "Ok boys, let's move out!" He hopped in the turret, we climbed in and sat down on the steel benches in the back; it was a tight fit with each of us having guns, body armor, and pockets bulging with ammo.

Private Young closed the hatch and moved us into the convoy; we rolled out the front gate.

The commander came over the speaker in the back with the marine song blaring over his voice singing his little rendition of the song again.

"From the Halls of Montezuma

To the shores of Tripoli;

The Army wins our countries battles

While we cower in the air, land, and sea."

Everyone laughed and yelled, "Fuck yeah! We're always in the shitter because of them. Always saving their ass!" Like clockwork, 'Who Let the Dogs Out' played loud over the speaker.

On the way, Sergeant Hunter went over our mission, "Alright gentlemen, listen up. We are to flush out the enemy in the catacombs and eliminate any threat. Anyone in the kill zone is free game. We'll be clearing crypts, tombs, and blowing tunnels when we find them. Same mission since the start of this operation, Hooah?"

"Hooah!" we hollered.

"Martinez and B, you'll take turns up on the .50 cal rifle to take out those filthy bastards in the towers."

"Yes, Sergeant."

We drove through the same crowd of people as usual. They were white on the screen waving their arms, yelling and throwing stuff. A couple rounds hit the side of the Bradley and I jumped.

B smiled and Martinez snickered.

"Huh, you'll get used to that," Hunter said. "You ever clear a building before?"

"No Sergeant," I said.

"Ok well, you'll get to clear a fuck load today. Follow my lead; shoot anything that moves and we'll be safe. These fuckers like to pop up outta nowhere, so be looking everywhere."

"Roger Sergeant, I will."

We slowly came to a stop, then the back dropped open and heat rushed in. "Ok, boys. Stay safe out there," the lieutenant piped over the speaker. The sun was shining bright off the crypts in the graveyard. I would be lying if I said I wasn't scared shitless; who wouldn't be. From the way this fight was going, there's a high likelihood of one of us being shot; it could be me. On the way out, Sergeant Hunter grabbed an AT-4 missile launcher and handed it to me with a smile, "Just in case." I strapped it around my shoulder and let it hang from my back. Rodriguez strapped a large black bag holding the .50 cal sniper rifle to his back. I pulled my pack tight then held my rifle up and walked out. With this gear and ammo on, I must have had at least an extra hundred pounds weighing me down. The Bradley closed when we were all out, leaving us exposed on a dirt path into the graveyard.

"Alright," Hunter said, "let's move out." We spread out and walked into the cemetery with guns raised. The graves were above ground; varying in range between three to five feet tall. They were made of brick and mortar, tan in color. New ones along with shattered ones; some were blown up with bones spewed all over the ground. I didn't know how they even got the bodies inside; my guess was that they must fold them up when they put them on the slab; I don't know.

B asked Hunter if we could stop so he could adjust his scope. Sergeant called back to the lieutenant, who gave us the go ahead. B set his M249 SAW light machine gun on top a grave and took aim at a crypt. He fired a couple rounds then adjusted. The lieutenant fired a couple rounds to adjust as well.

Sergeant Hunter ordered us to move out again and we slowly crept through the cemetery with our weapons raised. All of a sudden two rounds ripped past my head. Martinez yelled, "shit!" and dropped the ammo can as we all hit the ground. We heard a couple more shots zip past as Hunter yelled at Martinez to call back to the lieutenant to see if the Marines were firing at us. Things went silent; "Negative," the lieutenant said; "it's not them."

We took a knee behind a row of graves, "Something hit the ammo can." Martinez said.

"I wonder if it's a sniper?" Rodriguez said.

Martinez crawled over to the ammo canister and snatched it up quickly getting back to cover. He turned the can around showing two holes coming out from the side of the can. He opened it up and smoke came out. He looked inside to see a couple empty shells.

"Oh fuck man!" said Martinez. "They fucking went off. It must be the heat, shit." Everyone was silent. I couldn't help but to think about the grenades and rounds in my pockets going off; I wonder if everyone else was too. Hunter reported back to the lieutenant on what happened. We stood up and made our way to the first tomb.

"Alright Boney, pay close attention these first couple clears, I want you switching with me in a bit."

"Roger Sergeant."

B and I pulled guard in the rear while the rest of the squad cleared tombs. Martinez took the lead with Sergeant Hunter second. He kicked in the door then Sergeant Hunter fired a shot from his shotgun. Rodriguez and Martinez ran in firing while Sergeant Hunter rushed in after them. It looked simple; my heart was racing as we kept watch behind them; I heard weapons fire coming from close by. They walked out. "Empty," Hunter said.

We went on to the next. All of sudden a horrific smell filled the air.

"What the fuck is that?" I said.

"Must be a dead body baking in the heat," B replied.

We walked up to a cracked door and the smell got stronger, I tried holding my breath because I felt like gagging.

"I'll check it out." Martinez kicked the door open. "Oh fuck, definitely a dead body." He started gagging. Hunter went in with him; they both came back out in seconds. "We don't see it but there's a hole in there; must have died in the tunnel." Hunter said, "Oh, I can't stand that smell."

After pulling the tape off of two grenades, Sergeant Hunter held his breath and went back in to blow the tunnel. He ran back out gagging as the explosion went off sending dirt clouds through the air.

"Fuck, that's horrible," he said. "Alright, let's keep moving."

He cleared a few more tombs before handing me his shotgun and ordered me to clear with Rodriguez in lead. We slowly crept tomb to tomb; each one I cleared gave me more confidence that I could hold my own. We came to a little brown tomb with a rusty metal door that was unbolted. Rodriguez kicked in the door and shots flew out toward us, sounding like hornets as they zipped past my head. I managed to get a shot off before jumping back.

"Holy shit!" I yelled.

Sergeant Hunter and B fired rounds through the door. Martinez knelt outside the door and threw a grenade in. We stood back against the building.

Boom! A cloud of dust rushed out; Rodriquez and I stormed in firing; we let up halfway in. It was dark inside but I could see a hole in the ground. A cement block was taken out of the ground and placed beside the wall.

"Hole!" I yelled. We pointed our weapons at it.

"Blow it," Rodriguez told me. We both pulled out a grenade and threw them in. We ran out of the building as it blew. "Clear," we both said.

"Mighty fine job men," Hunter said. "Let's keep going.

*   *   *

We crept slowly through the maze of graves. Mounds of skulls and bones from blown down graves sometimes blocked our paths. We'd walk down a different row when possible. If not, we'd be forced to jump on top a grave to get to a position. I was sweating hard; it was so hot we had salt crusting all over our uniforms, making them stiff. If there was a hell, I'm sure this would be it.

I told everyone to drink water when I thought about it; last thing I needed was someone getting dehydrated and passing out. Rodriguez said, "Hydrate or die Doc" every time as if we were in basic.

In the middle of a water break we came under heavy fire. Multiple rounds screamed past and hit the wall right beside me; dust hit me in the face as I jumped to the ground behind a grave.

"Fucking shit, where's it coming from?" I shouted. Then I heard what sounded like a loud whistle.

"Stay down!" B yelled at everyone.

The crypt behind us exploded and covered me in dust and rocks. Rounds kept kicking up dirt and bouncing off the graves nearby.

"Two o'clock!" Martinez yelled.

I stood up and fired; squatted down again once the rounds started zipping by. Martinez radioed the lieutenant for support while we kept firing. Rodriguez and Hunter started advancing as we gave them cover fire.

When I stood and fired I saw guys with rags covering their heads peek around a headstone; a cloud of smoke spit up when they fired telling me I wasn't seeing things. I crouched back down and grabbed the AT-4 off my back. I hoisted it onto my right shoulder and released the safeties. B smirked at me, then suddenly stood up and fired. A second later I stood up and fired. It hit a crypt next to them in a huge explosion, blowing rocks and debris everywhere.

"Fuck yeah!" I heard B yell before he started firing his SAW again. I threw the launcher away and loaded a Frag into my M203 and I fired. *Thump! Boom!* Hunter and Rodriguez kept moving forward, hopping behind graves getting closer and closer to their position.

Our Bradley rolled up and started firing rounds downrange; graves and the sides of tombs shattered and crumbled down. We all advanced, firing as we ran forward. I had to jump on top of a grave to move ahead. When I went to jump off my feet went through and I slid to the ground. Bones and sand poured onto my lap, "Fuck man!" I jumped up quickly and moved forward. When we got to their position, they were gone.

"Fuck!" Sergeant Hunter screamed.

"Where the fuck are they? Fucking cowards!" Rodriguez yelled out.

"Let's clear the tombs," Hunter screamed. Hunter and Rodriguez ran into one while B, Martinez, and I went into the other. Martinez kicked in the door and I sprayed the room as we stormed in.

"Another fucking tunnel!" Martinez and I both untaped grenades, threw them in and jumped out. *Boom!*

"They're some slippery fucking bitches. Every fucking time," Hunter yelled. "Fuck!" He kicked a nearby grave.

I was pissed too; I couldn't believe they got away again; bunch of cowards.

"Tell the lieutenant to mow these buildings down," Hunter ordered Martinez. He radioed to the Bradley. A minute later it came rolling over through the cemetery. We stood back while they pushed both buildings over; they both crumbled down fast.

Chapter 16: Hit

I stood in back of the Bradley, staring in the mirror as we waited to move – desert camo's, green vest, M16, Oakley's, and a tan handkerchief tied around my face. It didn't look like me; I looked like death. I bet that's what they think when they see us coming; hope so, because death is the only thing I want them to see.

Only my third patrol out and I feel changed, different. I'm not afraid of being hurt; it feels inevitable. No pain, no gain, right? If I fall, hopefully someone can save my life. I've pushed all feeling out other than anger. Anger at the fact that this shit isn't over yet. The fact the enemy keeps getting the jump on us. I'm stuck in a recurring nightmare; day after day in hell, dodging bullets, shooting at demons and ghosts. My muscles are sore, my joints and back ache; most times I don't know where I get the energy to keep moving.

When the door dropped we walked out on full alert. We had started clearing tombs when I heard a gunfight break out across the street where another squad was.

A low thumping sound came up from behind me. A small black chopper shot past, it was flying low and fast. The barrels on its side started spinning, spitting out smoke; seconds later I heard the shots echo through the cemetery. It pivoted in a small circle over the cemetery as it shot. Once it stopped firing it turned away and quickly flew off. *Got em!* I thought, quietly hoping they didn't miss their mark. *One less guy we have to worry about.*

"Alright, let's stop here," Hunter said as we walked up to the back of a tan crypt.

"Martinez, I want you up top. Boney, you go with him to guard."

"Hooah," we both said.

I took off my gear, threw my aid-bag down and gave my weapons to Hunter. Rodriguez helped Martinez assemble the .50 cal. When it was ready I helped push Martinez up the side of the building. We handed him the rifle and some ammo, then I climbed up, reached down, and grabbed the SAW from B. We slowly crawled over to the edge of the roof. I took position a couple feet from him on the edge of the building where I could see in all directions. He took off his headgear and put on his hat. Then he took aim through the scope and started scanning the buildings downrange.

I was looking around at the cemetery, keeping close watch on the tombs around us. I kept hearing random shots; but I couldn't see anyone. Minutes later I heard Martinez say, "Found you, you mother fucker." He adjusted his scope then called to the lieutenant.

"Base 2 this is Halo 1"

"Halo 1 this is Base 2."

"Yeah I've got eyes on two guys in a building 600 meters in front of me. Looks like spotters popping their heads up looking through binoculars. Can I engage?

After a minute the lieutenant said, "Engage, light them up."

He took a deep breath then pulled the trigger. *Boom!* It was super loud, kicking out a cloud of smoke. Martinez kept the rifle steady with his eye on the scope, "Gotcha bitch," I heard him say. "Oh no you don't." He shot a couple more rounds before stopping.

"Base 2, I know I got one of them. I don't know about the second. I don't see any more movement."

"Roger that Halo 1."

He went back to scanning. Suddenly bullets started screaming past. I tried to see where they were coming from when a couple rounds hit the side of roof were my head was, kicking up dirt; I ducked down fast.

We were pinned on the roof as rounds zipped overhead. I waited until Martinez put his vest and helmet back on then we started crawling to the back of the building. Mortars landed around us, shaking the building. We got to the back and the guys were looking up waiting on us with hands raised. We tossed our weapons down then jumped over the side. I landed on my back; a shockwave of pain radiated from my mid-back to my ribs. I jumped up and put the rest of my gear on before we all ran back to a crypt we had cleared earlier to wait out the rest of the attack.

I told everyone to drink water as we sat on the floor drained, sweating, and panting. We all started to laugh. I didn't know why. Martinez started; it was infectious. We sat and talked about what just happened; Martinez was going on about his kills.

After a couple minutes the lieutenant told us to move out, so we went and started clearing crypts. We saw one with a door cracked open. Hunter pointed to Rodriguez and me to go clear it. We crept low, maneuvering around graves until we got to the side of the building. I pulled out a grenade, untaped it, and let the clip fly. After I counted three seconds I threw it into the door and backed off, *Boom!* Rodriguez and I rushed in shooting; no one.

We heard gunfire and rushed back outside to see B, Hunter, and Martinez shooting at a crypt; we joined in. Hunter and Martinez made their way up to the door, kicked it in and fired a round of shots.

"A fucking tunnel again!" Hunter yelled, "Rat bastards; I fucking hate'em."

It was the same worn out scenario. We get shot at, we shoot back, advance, and nothing. Even though we had eyes on people as we shot them down, the only thing we'd find were pools of blood. My only guess is they drag the bodies underground and leave them to die. I'll never forget the smell of rotting flesh and gunpowder. Sergeant Hunter looked at his watch and called over to the lieutenant to see if it was ok for us to stop and eat lunch. "Ok, let's find a building to take a break."

We found a tomb not too far away, cleared it and went inside. It wasn't big, maybe 100 square feet. There was a white marble casket on top a pillar in front of an open window, giving us a little protection.

B stood guard by the door while we ate. We all fell on the ground; exhausted, hungry, and on edge. I was nervous about setting my weapon down; someone could pop up next to us and send a missile through the window. But it looked like everyone else was ok with it. Martinez had his eyes closed, laying against the wall. I took out my MRE and ate cautiously, constantly looking through the window, trying to keep one hand on my rifle the whole time.

We all shared stories of where we grew up. Talking about how much we missed our friends and family back home. Martinez fell asleep, snoring with his MRE open at his feet. I wanted so bad to do the same thing, but I was too uncomfortable thinking we might come in contact at any moment.

I woke him up and told him to eat something quick because he needed the energy. He looked at me pissed so I said, "Whatever," and kept eating. He looked angry as he ripped open his food. I swore he was going to pass out while he ate, luckily he didn't. When Rodriguez was finished he switched out with B to give him a chance to eat.

"Ok," Hunter said, "I think we need to start covering more ground at one time. We're going to throw the .50 cal up top while the rest of us clear buildings. That way there would be a less likelihood of someone popping up without us knowing."

The Bradley started shooting down range, startling all of us. The lieutenant came over the radio, "Ok gentlemen, break's over. Time to get back to work." We all got our gear on and left the building.

As soon as we stepped out bullets ripped past my head; I jumped to the ground and heard a rocket scream over me; it exploded behind me. I couldn't believe they got on top of us that quickly; must have been waiting for us to walk out. It felt like there was no end to this shit.

B yelled, "10 o'clock," and we all let loose. I was used to being in the shit by now; my heart didn't jump when rounds passed. I just got super pissed, wanting to kill whoever was on the other end of my rifle.

My weapon felt like an extension of my hand; I could see now why they called it hand-to-hand combat. With every round I shot I could feel the impact on the other end; it was like I was punching through walls, piercing through bodies. I felt powerful; as long as I had my weapon, nothing could stop me.

I stuck a frag in the launcher and waited for Hunter and B to start shooting. Then I stood up with my weapon downrange. When I saw the towel heads above the graves, I pulled the trigger. *Thump! Boom!* It hit the side of a headstone, sending rocks and a large cloud of smoke into the air.

"Wooo! That's what I'm talking about, Fuck yea!" The guys cheered. We started advancing, taking turns laying cover fire. They didn't seem to be firing back as much. By the time we got to their position they were gone. There was only blood splattered on the ground where they had been.

"Fuck yeah! We got one," Hunter cried out.

"They're like fucking ghosts ma-" I was cut short when bullets started zipping by again. "Fuck!"

Mortar rounds started landing around. I jumped to the ground behind a grave; it shook hard with each explosion. Martinez called to the lieutenant. "We need fucking assistance. We're getting fucking slammed!"

The mortars stopped, but the firing got heavier and heavier; I thought it would never end. We tried sticking our heads up but we couldn't see where it was coming from before we were forced down again. A black chopper flew over our heads firing. I got up to see a tomb about 50 meters from us get shredded; half of the building ended up caving in.

"Fucking finally, bet they didn't get away from that one," Rodriguez said. We all laughed then got up and advanced on it.

*   *   *

We came up to a partly bombed out building, when Sergeant Hunter stopped us.

"Ok, B and Boney. Get up top."

The building was a little bigger than a tomb; two story with the top floors blown off. We walked around it to see if there was a spot where we could get pushed up top. There were pad locks on all the doors so we couldn't get up from the inside.

We found a hole blown out of the wall next to the street. We decided to climb in. Martinez and Rodriguez put together the sniper rifle while Hunter and I hoisted B up. He looked around and said it was a good spot. We passed up the .50 cal and the SAW. Then I climbed up. We ended up inside the only enclosed room up top; the rest of the building was blown down into the lower level.

B took the lead into the next room, crouching low, making sure no one saw us. We made our way to the front of the building by balancing and walking on top the first story walls. When we crawled to a room with a balcony we positioned ourselves on the edge.

I set the SAW on the ledge and started scoping out the cemetery. All I could see were graves and crypts surrounding us. There was a tree sitting in front of us with a few leaves on its branches; a black scarf hung from one of them.

I could see tall buildings in the city leading to a blazing gold dome in the distance: the Iman Ali Shrine. A couple shots went off in front of us. I looked around to see if I could spot where they came from with no success.

A couple minutes into it B called in targets down range. Once he got the go ahead, he fired.

"Got one," he called in, "I can see the other two moving around." He fired four more times then giggled. "Bet they're thrilled," he commented, then laughed. I laughed with him. He looked toward me, "You want to give it a try?"

"Fuck yeah!" I switched weapons with him, took my helmet and vest off and lay down. I slid the rifle onto my shoulder and looked through the scope. There were crosshairs with a red dot in the middle giving me a clear two hundred yard focus. I started scanning the buildings downrange. A minute later I saw a flash; a glare like the sun bouncing off glass.

I moved the scope over to the window of a crypt. Someone poked their head up from behind a grave, popped a shot off then got back down.

I set the cross hairs on the top portion of the slab, waiting for him to pop up, then called it, "Halo 1 to Base 2."

"Base 2 go ahead."

"I've got eyes on a target about 150 yards out. Is it ok to engage?"

"Engage, engage; light him up."

I took a breath in and took aim. Once the guy stuck his head up above my crosshairs, I pulled the trigger. *Bang!* My sight was knocked off; the kick was huge. Once I got my sight back on target I saw a big hole and the top of the slab knocked off. All I could make out were dirty rags fluttering in the wind behind the grave.

"Did you get'em?" B asked.

"Not sure; I think I did. No one's moving. Something's laying on the ground."

"Well fuck, you must have then; let me see."

I handed over the rifle and directed him to the spot, "Yeah someone's laying there; nice shot doc."

"Thanks," I said, before he went back to scanning the buildings. Sergeant Hunter popped up next to us, standing up above the wall.

"Ok, let's wrap it up and take a break, boys." As soon as I looked back at him a bullet screeched past my head. Then I heard a soft thud. Sergeant Hunter dropped off the wall to the lower level and screamed out in pain, "I'm hit!"

Chapter 17: Danger

Bullets rattled the wall behind me, spraying chunks of rock and dust into the air. B was trying to stick his head up and look out but kept falling back flat on the ground when the rounds went pinging off the cement around us. The only thing I could do was picture the sergeant bleeding out to death.

Shit! I thought, *I've gotta get over to him, what the fuck*. I slapped B on the shoulder.

"I'm climbing over to Hunter! Give me cover fire." I handed him the SAW and crawled across the floor. B planted the SAW on the roof and fired down range swearing and screaming. I was pinned down again when I came to the drop off; bullets ripped through the air above my head.

"Fuck!" I yelled, and then threw myself over the edge, landing hard on my side; knocking the wind out of me. I pushed myself up, and ran over to Sergeant Hunter, who was lying on the ground twisting and moaning. Blood was seeping out of his right shoulder. He was covered in dust.

I radioed to Martinez on my way over to him, "I need my bag and a Medivac. Sergeant is down. We're by the blue door near the street."

"On my way" Martinez radioed back.

I fell onto my knees next to Hunter, "I'm here Sergeant; let me take a look at you."

He moved his hands off his shoulder; I tore open vest and blouse. "You feel hurt anywhere else?"

He shook his head, "No, just my shoulder." I looked him up and down to see if he got hit anywhere else like I was trained.

"Here!" I heard Martinez yell from behind the door. I looked up to see the bag fly up and over the door, landing on the ground. I ran over and grabbed it then ran back to the sergeant.

I took the scissors from my bag and cut his shirt open; a bullet hole the size of a quarter was blown into his shoulder. Blood was slowly running out from the sides. I broke open a field bandage and pressed it on top of the wound. Martinez was trying to kick down the door without any luck.

"Here hold this tight and don't let go," I said, placing his hand on the bandage. The door had a metal chain looped through it and was padlocked. Martinez and I both tried kicking it open but it wouldn't budge. We would need bolt cutters to get through the lock. Mortars started landing, scaring the piss out of me.

"How the fuck are we going to get out of here? Does the Bradley have a chain to tear the fucker off?" I yelled at Martinez.

"No!" he screamed. "There's nothing!"

"Fuck!" I shouted, kicking the door. The ground shook underneath me over and over again; the explosions sounded close. I couldn't think of anything but going back up top and jumping off.

"We're going back over!" I yelled, "Give us cover while we jump off the other side!"

Martinez gave me a nod, "Shit, ok!" He radioed the lieutenant to help give us cover.

I ran back over to the sergeant, radioing B, "I need you to help me with Hunter!"

"Roger that!" he replied.

"We're going to have to go back up!" I yelled to the sergeant. "There's no other way out!"

He looked pale and frightened, "You ok?"

"Yeah, man. Fuck," he tiredly replied. I tied his bandage the best I could and closed his vest. After I got him to his feet B yelled down to us, "Ok!" holding his hand over the edge. I handed B the sergeant's rifle then lodged my pack up top. Next, I crouched against the wall with my hands clasped together and boosted Hunter up. He grabbed B's hand and I pushed him until he was over the edge.

After a moment B reached down for me. I got a running start and scaled the wall grabbing his hand. With his help I pulled myself up; bullets zipped past as I dragged my body over the edge. All three of us were now up top hugging the floor.

With the mortars landing closer I knew it was only a matter of time before they started hitting the building. Rounds were bouncing off the wall, blocking the way we originally came up. We figured the only way down was to walk across the top of the wall we just climbed and jump off; like walking across a balance beam in clear view of the enemy. There wasn't a floor on either side of us so we would take the chance of getting shot and ending up back were we started, trapped. But there weren't any other options.

"Ok," B said, "I'll help Hunter while you lay down cover fire."

"Ok! Let me know when you're ready!" I grabbed the SAW then crawled over to the edge of the building. B strapped the rifle on his back and grabbed the ammo. On the count of three I started relentlessly firing downrange.

Once Hunter and B made it to the edge and jumped off, I strapped my bag on then shot a couple more rounds downrange. After slinging the SAW over my shoulder I took a second to pray:

Please don't let me die; I don't want to get shot. After a count of three I jumped up and started across. "Shit. Fuck this shit," was the only thing I was thinking and said as rounds zipped past me. I tried my best not to fall off as mortars shook the wall. My heart sank when I almost slipped off, causing me to stop for a second. I felt like one of those ducks in a carnival game, running in clear view, hoping to not get shot.

"Shi-i-t!" I yelled as I jumped off the side of the building, landing hard on my legs next to a grave. My right knee popped, causing me to collapse in pain. I looked up to see a grave only yards away blow up from a mortar; another one exploded close by a second after. I forced myself up and ran over to B and Hunter. On the way a mortar hit the ground a couple feet from me and didn't go off.

"Shit!" I screamed, jumping to the side. When I got to Hunter I threw his arm over my shoulder and started running. Rodriguez came around the corner of the building firing downrange then waved us over to him. We ran to the front of the building and jumped inside through a doorway inside a small room. Each of us hugged the walls in the shadows on either side. I watched as bullets zipped through the doorway and rattled the brick wall, shooting clouds of dust into the beam of light shining in.

Mortar rounds landed all around; the blasts shook the building, engulfing the room with dust and smoke. I thought the building was going to fall in on us as they came pounding in. Bullets kept hitting the wall between us, making Rodriguez and me jump back. We were trapped; there was no place to go.

Rodriguez was terrified; his face scrunched up as if fear was causing him pain. My body shook harder with every explosion; it felt like my brain was shaking against my skull. I closed my eyes and saw flickering lights. Suddenly a warm vibrating sensation ran through my body; I started reciting the Lord's Prayer in my mind. *Our father in heaven...*

My grandma appeared in front of me, her face an array of different colors: Purple, white, blue and orange. We were engulfed in darkness. She rocked in her chair moving back and forth praying. A bright orange light shone on me as we prayed together, eliminating the darkness we were in. It was warm and peaceful, wrapping me with comfort. All my fear and pain were taken away, filling me with nothing but joy and love.

I heard explosions and felt the ground shake, but it was in a separate place. It was almost as if I were in both places at once. The thought crossed my mind that I died. My whole life was in front of me; it seemed like time was non-existent. I stood next to my grandma waiting, not knowing what was going to happen next. I didn't care. Everything was going to be ok. It felt like I was there for hours, maybe days.

I heard tracks slamming against the pavement outside, its engine getting louder as it moved up the street outside. The Bradley's gun got louder as they got closer. Martinez was muffled as he spoke, "Come on; let's go!"

Everything disappeared. I was pulled back into the building as my eyes opened. Martinez popped two smoke grenades out the doorway for cover; thick red and yellow smoke filled the air. The medical track stopped and dropped its back hatch. Rodriguez and I lifted Hunter and ran him over to the track. Bullets came zipping by as we moved. We handed him off to the medic and threw his gear on the floor.

Martinez gave us cover fire while we ran back through the smoke, into the room. It sounded like our Bradley dozed over graves as it pulled up on the side of the building. I could hear bullets bouncing off its armor as it fired down range. We ran outside and jumped into the back.

The door slammed shut while the Bradley moved away; we watched the screen as white bodies darted away.

"Fuck!" Martinez kicked the metal seat before sitting down. We were all panting hard; I was worn out.

"Drink water." I said, tiredly lifting my canteen up to drink. As we sat I finished closing up my pack, making sure all the medical supplies were in the right spot. I made a mental note to pick up an aid-bandage when we got back to base. When I went to close the pouch it was in, there were two small holes punched through it. I stuck my finger through them; it went clean through.

"Shit," I said, tapping Rodriguez. He opened his eyes and looked at me.

"Look at this shit man; I can't believe I got that close to getting hit."

"Shit bro. I think we all got lucky. That shit was close."

"Yeah man, I know."

I sat back and closed my eyes, wanting so badly to go to sleep, but my mind kept racing. Thoughts about the guy I shot, how close I came to getting shot and the bright lights. What was that? It felt like I had died back in that room. How do I know I didn't? I was going to say something about it before the lieutenant's voice came blasting over the radio.

"Alright boys! Gotta go back out in 5."

"Fuck man I'm tired!" Rodriguez shouted back. There was no response. I didn't want to go back out, especially with a man short. B was lying back with his eyes closed shaking his head. We sat in silence for a minute; the only sound was the motor of the main gun moving around looking for targets. When I thought about Sergeant Hunter again I remembered something funny and started giggling.

"What's so funny?" said B. "I'd like to hear something funny right about now in this shithole."

"Did you guys hear Sergeant's voice?" I asked; "he sounded like a little girl."

I squeaked in a high-pitched voice, "I'm hit." Everyone laughed. That opened up a doorway for more shits and giggles; it was like everyone needed to joke around to keep our minds off of going back out. Martinez took charge of the team since he had seniority. We were one man short and no one else was coming out to replace Hunter. We had enough firepower to keep going, so we filled our water and restocked ammo. The back door dropped open.

"Ok guys. Watch your six out there."

Chapter 18: Worn Out

None of us wanted to keep going, but we had no choice. We took a quick break in a tomb to rehydrate. I squatted to the ground and finished drinking my third bottle of water for the day. My DCU's were covered in salt crystals and dirt. It had been two weeks since I'd showered and shaved. I was so exhausted I could have passed out. I've never been worked this hard in my entire life and there was no end in sight. At times I felt like being dead would be a better option.

"Who's up for a little target practice?" Martinez asked. Everyone chuckled except me; I must have missed the joke.

Martinez explained to me that we were going to try and lure people out with bait. Two people had to go out and start making commotion while the other guys watched for the enemy.

"Ok, pick a number between 1 and 20," Martinez said.

I said 13; his number was 15.

"Damn," Rodriguez and I both said; then we looked at each other. He smiled, "Gotta die someday, right?"

"Yeah, buddy." Martinez said, "Don't worry; they can't shoot worth shit anyway."

"Glad it's not me," B stated before walking through the doorway to outside.

Rodriguez and I stood on top of newer graves in front of the tomb, in clear view for anyone in the cemetery to see. My heart started pounding, filling me with a burst of adrenaline. I've survived crazy shit all day; I should already be dead. Rodriguez started yelling, "Woohoo! Yeah!"
I joined in, the whole time moving my head scanning the cemetery for people who might come out to look.

Rodriguez pointed to the top of a tomb in the distance, "You think I can hit the nipple on the top there? The blue one?"

"Bet you I can before you," I said.

B and Martinez spread out, watching for weapons fire. Rodriguez took a frag out and popped it into his grenade launcher. After taking a couple seconds aiming, he fired. Thump! It sizzled downrange and exploded off to the side of it.

"Damn!" he yelled, I laughed while loading a round. I took aim and popped it off. Boom! The building next to it exploded.

"Fuck man!" I yelled loud, trying to draw attention. Rodriguez shot again and hit it. I pointed to another one, "The blue and yellow dome there."

There was a building in my way as I aimed, so I jumped on top of a taller grave and fired. The top of the dome caved in.

"Fuck yeah!" I shouted.

As Rodriguez took aim to fire another one, bullets started flying around us; we jumped down as B yelled, "Three!" I stood up firing.

When I squatted down again, Rodriguez yelled at me, "Frag'em!" So I loaded a round, counted to three and stood up. I saw two people shooting; one in grey rags, another in black. I aimed and pulled the trigger, *Thump!*

The round launched out and hit the tree right behind them. *BOOM!* It split in half, sending smoke and debris everywhere; I saw the guys fall.

"Fuck yeah! Yeah!" Everyone screamed.

"Yeah! Nice shot," B yelled at me.

We started advancing towards them. Two of us laid down suppressive fire while the other two sprinted forward, leaping behind another grave. When I went to rush forward, there were a couple of graves knocked down in a pile blocking my way. I ran and jumped on top shooting; then jumped back down.

I looked over and saw that Rodriguez had to do the same, but when he jumped on a grave his foot went through. He fell headfirst trying to get it unstuck. I ran over and helped him get his foot unstuck. We both started laughing because he was on his head with his legs dangling in the air.

We got a couple graves away when the firing got heavier. Rodriguez took a grenade out and tried throwing it, but it slipped from his hand, falling two feet in front of him.

"Grenade!" he yelled; we both jumped behind a grave as it went off. *BOOM!*

I tried throwing one, but as my arm came forward it felt like I was throwing a 40-pound weight and it just rolled out of my hand.

"Grenade!" *BOOM!*

After it went off we laughed that none of us had enough strength to lodge grenades. I looked back at B, who gave us a go-ahead before firing off a bunch of rounds. We jumped up and made our final push forward. I was filled with a rush of adrenaline as we came up on their positions. The only thing I saw was blood sprayed over the ground when got there.

Fucking got the bastards, I thought. Rodriguez pointed to his eyes then to a blood trail on the ground. It looked like someone had been dragged into a tomb. He pointed to the building. I nodded.

I took lead, quietly creeping towards the building. When we got to the door I took out a grenade and threw it in. After it exploded, Rodriguez kicked the door in and we stormed in firing. No one was inside, but it was filled with rocket launchers, mortar shells, and bullets; a weapons cache.

"We hit gold," Rodriguez said.

Before I could respond a hole in the ground came into my view.

"Hole!" I yelled pointing my weapon at it. Rodriguez grabbed two grenades out of his pocket and threw them in. We walked outside as they went off. *BOOM!*

Rodriguez called the lieutenant to let him know about the weapons.

"Blow the shit," the lieutenant ordered us. "If you can't, I'll push the building over."

"Roger that," Rodriguez replied. "Keep watch while I blow this bitch," he said, walking past me into the doorway

"Got it," I said.

I stood behind a large pillar next to a wall across from the door, a perfect position to take cover from the blast and still keep watch of the area. I waved to B who was with Martinez 30 yards away. He waved back and kept scanning the cemetery. Rodriguez took out a grenade, threw it in and ran out as it went off. *BOOM!*

"Fuck! They didn't blow." Rodriguez stated after walking back in. He came out and stood directly across from the door and shot a grenade in with his launcher. *BOOM!* The building exploded multiple times sending smoke and debris everywhere before it collapsed in.

Bullets started flying past me. I fell behind the pillar while rounds rattled the wall behind me. Neither of us could see where it was coming from so we called it in. After a couple seconds we heard the lieutenant start lighting someone up; the Bradley's gun was distinguishable from any other weapon. It pulled up a couple graves away from us. We jumped up and fired downrange while we ran over to the Bradley and jumped in.

I fell into the bench exhausted and panting. Rodriguez and I looked at each other, then bumped fists. We both sat trying to catch our breath and drink water. I just happened to look down and see that he was bleeding from his left leg.

"Dude, you're hit," I said, pointing. "What happened?"

He grabbed his leg and looked at it. There was a blood soaked hole in his pants. I made him take off his boot and pull up his pants. He had taken a piece of shrapnel in the shin. I took a field bandage out of my pack, opened it, and held pressure on the leg.

"Dude, I might have to send you back." I said.

"Fuck no doc, I'm ok," he said desperately.

I stared him in the eyes, not wanting him to get more injured by going out. "Are you sure?"

"I'm serious, it doesn't even hurt," he said. My leg started throbbing in pain; at that moment I knew how he felt. I should have said something about it but I didn't want to leave; we still had a fight to win.

I held pressure on it for a couple minutes and saw the bleeding had gone down. Rodriguez begged me to not send him back; he stared me in the eyes.

"Please doc, those bastards are still out there. We've gotta kill them for Hunter." I didn't say anything; that's been my driving factor since he got hit. I wrapped the bandage around his leg and told him to put his boot back on so I could see how he was with weight on it.

He stood up and walked around, "See, I don't feel a thing. I'm good." He wasn't limping, so I told him, "Ok, but we have to get it looked at when we get back. Tell me if it gets worse."

"Thank you bro," he said. "I'll tell you, promise."

*   *   *

Rodriguez and I were scanning the cemetery on top of a tomb. B and Martinez were out clearing buildings in front of us. Minutes after getting into position, something moved in a building off to my left. I swung the SAW over ready to fire, but stopped short on pulling the trigger when I noticed a marine uniform. We both stared hard at each other through our scopes, trying to figure out if we were friend or foe; I could see him biting his lip. I would have to shoot him if he started firing; friendly fire is a motherfucker. *'What the fuck do I do?'* was the only thought racing through my head.

I slid my finger off the trigger and pointed the muzzle in the air then smiled at him. He did the same, slowly waving back before disappearing inside the dark room. I went back to scanning, nearly pissing my pants with how close that was.

I noticed that I couldn't see B or Martinez; they must have gone in a building. All of a sudden I heard weapons fire, then I saw B and Martinez shuffle into view, shredding up the side of the building with their weapons before going out of view again.

My heart was pumping because I couldn't give them cover fire; why the fuck didn't they stay in sight? I wanted to jump down and give them support.

"What the fuck is that?" Rodriguez asked.

"I think they came in contact. I only saw them for a few seconds over there." I pointed over towards a building on our left.

"Can't get a clear view," he said. After looking through his scope, he said, "They ok?"

"I don't know, call'em," I said.

We heard a couple more shots as he radioed to see if they needed help. No one answered back. It went silent for a minute as another couple explosions went off.

"No, we're good. Heading back over," Martinez radioed back. I saw them creeping back between the graves towards our building. At that moment we came under heavy fire; rounds flew overhead forcing us down. We put our helmets back on and climbed over towards the back of the building; we threw our weapons down to B and Martinez, then jumped.

Trying not to land on my bad leg, I landed on my side onto the edge of a blown-over grave, knocking the wind out of me. As I was standing up a little black chopper flew overhead with barrels blazing; firing at whoever the fuck was shooting at us.

"Fuck yeah! Kill'em!" B yelled.

"Oh shit!" Martinez said excitedly, "let's get a good view of the city."

We followed him around the building and took cover. "What's up man?" I asked.

"We're going to drop a bomb on one of the hotels."

It got eerily quiet; I could tell operations had stopped by the silence. It was almost too peaceful. I heard one or two gunshots before Rodriguez pointed up to the sky, "There it is!"

When I looked up a black plane came jetting across the sky over us towards the city. Once it got over one of the tall buildings, a black dot fell out and sunk into one; I saw smoke blow out of the top windows. Five seconds later it went up in a huge explosion from the middle sending dust and smoke everywhere.

It toppled over; crumbling down until there was nothing left except a cloud of smoke lingering in the sky.

"Dude...that was nuts!" I said, "Fucking awesome." All of us cheered.

"That's what I'm talking about!" B screamed.

All of a sudden we were blown back from a rush of wind. The sound of the explosion was faint; I heard the whole thing happen again from beginning to end. A loud grumble filled the air and the ground shook hard from the explosion. We took out a whole building in a matter of seconds.

"Forty-two confirmed kills? Fuck yeah!" Martinez yelled. We all cheered, giving each other hi-fives, celebrating a victory. We started clearing buildings again with a renewed sence of winning. I don't know how my body kept pressing on, but I was glad I had enough strength to keep moving forward.

An hour later Martinez stopped us again. We watched as another bomb obliterated a tall building to dust. Fifty-five confirmed kills. It felt like we were finally winning this thing.

Minutes later the lieutenant called us back in. Our shift was over for the day; earlier than usual. We all ran back to the Bradley and hopped in. I collapsed into the seat from the weight of my gear, happy the day was over. We were beat up; dirt, salt, and sand covered our bodies. I was going to pass out on the way back. My knee was swollen and it hurt badly. Everyone was roughed though; I wasn't a special case. I'm not stopping until I get shot or end up dead. To me, pain is less important.

Chapter 19: The Raid

Sergeant Hunter woke me up in the middle of the night, "Grab your gear and meet me outside." I was pissed because I was finally getting good sleep; I wondered what was going on. I threw my gear on and went outside.

It was pitch black out; artillery rounds were shooting through the air towards the city. I couldn't figure out what was going on. Our shift only ended six hours ago. We stopped next to the medic track; Sergeant Yates walked out the back.

"Private Boney," he greeted me.

"Sergeant"

"Ok, you've been reassigned to Sergeant Yates for tonight's raid," Hunter said. "I've gotta get back. Check you guys later." He ran off towards his vehicle.

"Alright, you have fun out there man?" he asked in his heavy southern accent.

"Fun's not the word." I said. "What's this raid about? Where are we going tonight?"

"Into the city; we're bringing the fight to those bastards to try to end this thing. Make sure you load up with ammo, we roll out in fifteen."

"Hooah Sergeant."

My weapon was clean and I was already loaded up with ammo, so I set my pack in the back and ran to take a piss. I sat in the back of the track for a minute and tried my best to fight off sleep while we waited.

Sergeant Yates walked in, "Ok men! Let's move out." Private Baker raised the back door and I popped open the top of the track and secured it down. I stood in the back using the bench to support my weight while we moved.

We headed out the front gate with "WHO LET THE DOGS OUT!" blaring over the radio. The only difference was that the commander wasn't talking. Everyone was dead quiet. We took a different route than normal, then went dark a mile or two away from base; all lights were turned off in the convoy. I brought my specs down in front of my eyes and switched them on. Everything I looked at was illuminated in green and white with black shadows. Suddenly, multiple loud explosions came rumbling past me. I looked over to see four white artillery shells bearing through the sky towards the city. The explosions got louder as we drove towards them. The vehicle started shaking from the tremors.

We turned a corner and the city of Najaf came into full view in the distance. When the shells impacted it sent up a big white flash; green and white flames burned surrounding buildings for a split second before disappearing.

We came up on a roadblock. Two Humvees, an M-1 tank, and two Bradlcy's were sitting in the middle of the road. There were five cannons lined up in the distance, shooting multiple shells off every minute. We went through the checkpoint and headed towards them.

When we stopped, the commander got out and walked over to someone standing next to the cannons watching the city through a pair of binoculars. They talked for a minute, placing a map on the front of a vehicle, pointing at different areas. He jumped back in the lead vehicle and we took off again.

After a half mile we turned onto a street that led us through a small row of houses. Eventually we ended up surrounded by piles of junk. I suddenly got a strong whiff of something rotting; it was horribly overwhelming. We were driving through some kind of dump, going around the side of the city to where the mosque was located; the golden dome was getting closer. The smell got stronger, more potent; I held my breath to stop myself from throwing up. I put my hand over the bandana on my face to alleviate some of the smell. After a minute or two I got used to it. The convoy came to a sudden stop and we sat for a few minutes.

"Yeah team leader this is Tango 1." A voice came over the radio, "It looks like a bunch of I.E.Ds are daisy chained together, blocking the road in."

"Roger Tango 1," another voice said. "Let's try to blow'em."

Gunshots rang through the air several times before multiple explosions went off, sending huge flaming balls into the air. *BOOM! BOOM! BOOM!* By the time the convoy moved forward again the artillery had stopped raining in.

After a minute, all hell broke loose. The only sounds were gunfire and explosions. Red and yellow tracer rounds flew through the night sky;

balls of fire floated into darkness with each explosion. My heart beat fast as we got closer to the action; the taste of iron filled the back of my throat.

Our vehicle turned out of the land field onto the road leading into the city. There were dirt hills on either side of us; flames were raging from piles of junk, I could feel the heat kissing my face as we passed. In fifty yards we were surrounded by dozens of small homes. A tank in front of us turned their barrel so it was about a foot away from the wall. Dirt and rocks flew out as it blew a round into the side; the house caved in a second. Tracer rounds came flying out of a house next to it, bouncing off the tank a few times; one came whizzing by my face. In a few seconds the tank turned and blew that house down too. If they weren't dead, they sure had to be hurt.

I suddenly felt numb. Everything from the light shining on the city to the tracer rounds and explosions turned bright and vivid; every noise sounded crisp, it felt like I had taken a drug. My pulse started racing; I was scared, and at the same time pumped, ready to jump into action.

After we turned another corner, troops started jumping out of the back of Bradleys and Humvees and stormed the surrounding buildings. I saw tracer rounds flying around inside through the windows. I started shooting at people firing down on us in the windows up high. A man popped up shooting behind a short wall. A Humvee gunner shot him down; then a soldier jumped out, ran over and threw a grenade on top him. It went off with a low thud as he ran back to the vehicle. Sergeant Yates started firing his Berretta at a tall building in front of us. Rockets started flying out of windows, hitting the sides of the tanks. They blew up in a ball of fire, leaving just a smudge of black on the side; I could feel the heat as each one went off. Bullets rained into the windows from the line a split second later. It felt like in a way, we were untouchable.

Another rocket flew out from behind a burning pile in the street and hit the side of a Bradley with a loud explosion. A huge ball of fire soared into the air; flames shot up from the supplies tied on the side. Multiple tracer rounds started bouncing off the Bradley; they were coming from multiple buildings. I shot back along with everyone else.

A soldier climbed out of the turret without a protective vest on. He took his jacket off and started hitting the flames trying to put it out. Rounds flew past him bouncing off the vehicle's armor. Another rocket flew past his head and exploded on the ground behind him.

I was hoping he wouldn't get hit, praying that I wouldn't have to get out and drag him to safety. Rounds went flying past my head; they started bouncing off our vehicle too. The shooting seemed to get heavier everywhere. All I could say was "Shit! Fuck this shit!" and Sergeant Yates kept yelling, "Fucking cock sucking maggots!" I fired at anything that moved in a window.

The soldier eventually got the fire out. On the way back to the turret he had to jump back and duck down as bullets hit around him, he crawled back into the turret safely. I let out a sigh of relief.

We pushed deeper into the city; another two blocks and we stopped. We sat in the open at the end of a street. The mosque was on my right and a row of buildings lined the street on my left. A pile of burning trash was blazing 20 yards in front of me.

The fight grew even more intense; I was changing my magazine every two or three minutes. People stuck their head out of a window and instantly got lit up. They started shooting at us behind the burning trash across from me. I remember thinking how great it was to have a big red cross painted on the side of us. If that didn't say shoot at me, what did. Bullets came screeching past me; I watching the red streaks fly by my head.

"Shit!" Sergeant Yates yelled real loud. I watched as he shot up at a building across from us; a couple other people shot up too. A body came falling out of a window several stories high. It landed with a crunch as it hit the ground headfirst. A gang of tracer rounds flew into it; some ricocheted off the ground back into the air. The body lay contorted and limp.

While I was looking for somewhere else to fire, a rocket shot out from behind the burning trash towards my head. I moved to the left as it came burning past my right side. The heat scorched my face as it soared by. A rush of adrenaline burst through me; on instinct I took aim at a figure behind the flames and opened fire. The first round dug deep into the middle of his chest. I felt relieved that I hit him as he fell. My heart raced as I saw someone dart out of a building and bend down to pick something up. As they stood I opened fire again, so did everyone around me. With my attention on the target, I didn't notice a Humvee driving up on my right. It stopped in front of us with the gunner's head in front of my weapon the second I reached the end of my magazine.

Shit! I thought. *A second earlier I would have hit him in the head.* I ducked down into the track and started gasping for air. *This is fucking crazy*! As I changed my magazine out, I looked up to see red and yellow tracer rounds flying over the opening like fireworks in the sky. I've been standing in that shit; I couldn't believe I haven't gotten hit by now.

After I got the magazine in, I gave myself the count of three then jumped up and started shooting at a building in front of me. The next thing I knew we started driving backwards. The tanks and Bradleys from the front started moving into the street in front of me. As we backed out the squads exited the buildings and jumped back in their vehicles.

We drove out back through the dirt hills and into the landfill. I thanked God that we got out safe. On the way out I didn't notice the smell of the trash; all I could smell was gunpowder and smoke. We headed back out past the artillery as they started hammering away at the city again. I watched the city as we drove back towards base, all lit up with fires blazing around. It was like the whole city was on fire. I hoped the bastards inside were all burning up so we could end this fight by morning.

Chapter 20: Hate

I was reassigned to a new squad the next night. They were throwing me wherever they needed me until the mission was over. It reminded me of basic, the way the drill sergeants changed PLs every time they made a mistake; a soldier has to get used to taking orders from anyone.

Sergeant Yates walked me over to my new squad leader and introduced me to the team. I noticed that Specialist Valerez, from the troop that survived the attack in the Bradley, was on the squad. He was quiet and just nodded to me when I said, "What's up." We rolled out the front gate as the sun was setting; no one talked. I stared at the ground thinking about the fight ahead. When will this shit end?

We sat in dead silence after we relieved the team. I waited for the hatch to drop, but it never did; we just sat looking at each other.

"Alright," the sergeant piped up. "I think we could all take a break tonight. There's zero visibility out; can't see shit anyway, even with our specs. Anyone disagree you can speak up now."

"Fuck, I'm ok with it," one of the soldiers said. We all agreed. It felt like a weight was lifted off my chest. After days of non-stop chaos, I think it was a much-deserved break.

"Alright, we'll go out and walk the street every hour or so, and let the lieutenant do most of the work for once."

"Fuck. Finally," Valerez muttered before closing his eyes and laying his head back. We sat in the Bradley driving up and down the road. I watched the screen most the time; every now and then a white figure would run in and out of buildings. When they sat still the lieutenant brought the cross hairs center mast and lit them up.

As the explosion from the gun rang through the inside, their bodies blasted into pieces, leaving a bright white splatter on the wall and ground that slowly faded to black as it cooled down. I wasn't ready the first time he shot; my eardrum was still throbbing from the blast. We got out of the Bradley and patrolled every hour or so. We walked up and down the street to make sure no one was around. We only went into the cemetery once to clear a building the lieutenant wanted us to check on.

The team next to us came in contact a couple times that night. I watched the cemetery light up, rockets flew through the air, exploding into huge fireballs. My heart started racing, imagining how intense the fight was. I knew it was Sergeant Hunter's team. I felt like running over to help, but we just listened to the radio, waiting on a call for assistance. It always ended before they needed help.

We were relieved from the line an hour after sunrise. When we got back to base I went straight over to the DEFAC for breakfast. On the way back over to the Bradley I heard people yelling. One guy threw his gear on the ground and kicked it, swearing and screaming; he was going on about someone surrendering.

When I got to the Bradley the lieutenant told us that the insurgents had made a ceasefire agreement. The soldiers out on the line were watching them walk right past as they surrendered and left the cemetery and mosque. No one was detained; we let all the murderers walk right past us.

I was pissed; we all were. Specialist Valerez started to scream, "What the fuck was the point if they just get to walk away! Huh?!" He cried and fell to his knees.

"Why did they have to die man, why? It should have been me…," he kept saying.

All of us went over and put our hands on him to try to calm him down; talk him through it. I felt his pain, this mission felt pointless. We didn't capture a single person responsible for killing our troops. How could they just let the same people killing us walk right by us without fault? I grew cold and empty inside; it felt like the lives we lost was for nothing. There is no justice in war.

The lieutenant ordered me to report back to Sergeant Bricks at the aid-station. The whole battle kept flashing through my mind on the walk over; the many times I was shot at, the people I saw die. The same thing kept running through my mind: *What was it all for?* I walked past a lot of guys who looked just as angry as me; scrunched up faces with their heads hanging low.

When I got back everyone was tearing down the aid-station; they were quiet as they moved stuff around.

"Reporting back, Sergeant Bricks," I said standing at ease.

"Alright, Boney. I heard you did well out there. Ready to go home?"

"Hoo-ah Sergeant. Ready as ever."

"Alright soldier, report to Sergeant Brown and help with the tear down. We should be heading out of this shithole by the end of the day."

"Yes, Sergeant."

I reported back to Sergeant Brown and helped with tearing down the tents and loading cots. Small tried talking to me while we worked. "You have fun out there?" he asked me. I gave him an empty stare. "It was nowhere near fun, dude."

"What, did you see any action?"

"I don't want to talk about it," I snapped back. His face turned deep red as he went quiet. He stopped talking to me; I think he got the hint that it's better forgotten.

Sergeant Brown was more quiet than usual. The only time she said anything was to give an order, and then she was distant, staring right through everything in deep thought.

"Dude, what's wrong with Sergeant Brown? She seems spooked," I asked Saul after Brown walked off to use the restroom.

"Oh…yeah, you weren't here when it happened."

"When what happened?" I asked.

"Two days ago we got mortared pretty hard. Everyone ran to get under the barricades. You know that guy she's been talking to since we got here?"

"Yeah, her old friend?" I finger quoted.

"Yeah, he was underneath a barricade when a mortar landed next to it, sending shrapnel through the opening. It sliced his head in half and he died.

"What?" I said shocked, "Dude, no joke?"

"Yup, she hasn't been the same; she cried the whole day yesterday."

"Fuck man, what are the odds of that happening? We aren't even safe under barricades. That's fucked up."

"Yup"

We got quiet when we saw her walking back. A couple hours later we were heading out the gates back to camp Victory. The whole ride my knee kept throbbing in pain. I figured it must have been sprained. When I thought back to how it happened, random images and feelings from the fight took hold of me.

I switched out with Saul halfway back to stretch out and get some rest. Nightmares kept waking me up in a cold sweat. I reached out for my weapon each time, being comforted that I had it close. One time I thought we were getting attacked because I heard gunfire, but it was only the belt buckle knocking against the wall. All I could think about was the blood trails, the smell of rotting flesh, hundreds of skulls and bones littered around the cemetery floor. I kept seeing the bones that fell on me when my foot went through a grave. It all felt surreal, like a bad dream, but I know it was real... I can't wait to get my clothes washed.

*   *   *

It was around 1900 hours when we rolled through the gate at North Victory. I never thought I'd be happy to see this place again, but I was. After everything I just went through, it was nice to feel like things would be back to normal again. I

243

couldn't wait to joke around with everyone, take a shower and get back to a normal routine.

We parked our vehicle in the motor pool and went to the CP to check in. After turning in our specs, Sergeant Flynn told us that we would have the next three days off to rest; all we needed to do was check in at morning formation every day.

Excited, I grabbed my stuff and started walking to my trailer. Everything from the past month had been racing through my head non-stop. I couldn't wait to get to my room and talk to Reynolds about it. I heard loud music and people laughing as I approached the trailer. It was nice to hear everyone and to be able to goof off for the first time in a while. I wondered what everyone would think once they found out what happened.

"Who the fuck – Boney! Yeoh! Whats up?" Reynolds said as I opened the door. He was sitting on his bed with an Xbox remote in his hand. Scott, Marc, and Jacob were sitting around playing as well.

"What's up guys? How's it going?"

"How's it going? You're the one that's been gone a whole month," Marc said.

"Yeah, where the fuck have you been?" Scott asked.

"I've been attached to the 1-5 Cavalry in Najaf. It's been fucking hell," I said. "Marc get the fuck off my bed; dude, what the fuck?"

"Ok, Ok. No need to get your panties in a bunch," he said sliding from the bed to the floor.

I tossed my gear on the floor and plopped down on my bed.

"Fuck this feels so good; I get to sleep in my own bed tonight, yes!"

Everyone laughed and went back to playing Halo.

"So what did you do the whole month?" Scott asked.

"I was on the front fucking line fighting insurgents, that's what," I said proudly.

"Ha-ha yeah right, you'd never get put on the front line," Marc said with a goofy smile. I wanted to punch him in the face.

"Yeah the fuck right. Dude, I was attached to a couple different teams doing patrols in a fucking cemetery."

"What was it like?" Scott asked.

"It was hell. We were clearing tombs running on top of graves and our feet would break through; we'd get covered in dust and bones. I even shot a couple people. It felt like a bad dream."

"You weren't on no front line, quit lying," Jacob said.

"Yeah, you probably were dreaming," Marc said arrogantly. Everyone laughed. I got pissed they were joking about it; *What the fuck? I'm trying to be serious; why did I need to lie. Why didn't they believe me?*

"Oh. It's fucking funny huh?" My head got light and dizzy. Everyone kept laughing. I couldn't believe how disrespectful they were being to me in my own room.

"WHO THE FUCK DO YOU THINK YOU ARE HUH! Get the fuck out my room!" I stood up and grabbed my weapon, "NOW! Get the fuck out!"

"Whoa, whoa. Calm down Boney. Chill." Reynolds jumped up and stood between us.

"You fucking heard me; get the fuck out of my room before I fuck you up." I looked directly at Marc, wanting to fucking shoot him in head. I was sweating hard; my heart was beating fast; *just give me a reason.*

"Alright, alright. Fuck, calm down," he said, holding his hands up on the way out the door.

"I'll show you fucking calm if I hear you talking shit again." I spit in his direction out the door, narrowly missing his shoulder.

"Ok, shit got serious. I'm out." Scott said. Everyone got up quickly and left. I slammed the door shut behind them.

"Fucking pricks," I said.

"Man you didn't need to do all that Boney. You should chill out, relax."

"Fuck you Reynolds. I don't care if you believe me or not," I said.

"Man whatever, fuck." He lay on his bed. "You want to play halo?"

I was still fuming inside. *What's the point of lying? I had nothing to gain from it. What happened was real; I can't get my mind off of it. Now I know how fast friends can become enemies; I'll never say shit to them again outside of work.*

"No, I'm good. I'm gonna shower; haven't taken one in weeks."

After getting my stuff unpacked I ran over to the showers. It was the first time cold water felt good to me. I closed my eyes and let it run over my head, daydreaming about being back home. *Four more months and I'll be back home.*

*   *   *

I'm different...changed in some way. I longed to be back out in the field doing patrols, being the combat medic I signed up to be. I was fed up with doing duties instead of real missions. My primary job lately was to escort Iraqis around while they emptied Port-a-potties; I hated it. Being around them made me uncomfortable. It was different before I left. I used to ride around and joke with them; even help with their English if they asked. Hell, I wasn't worried. I'd wear headphones and listen to music; sometimes even fall asleep.

Now... fuck, now I couldn't keep my eyes off them. I sat with my rifle loaded, finger on the trigger, ready to fire at any second. I'd stare at them the whole shift, waiting for them to do something a little off. I yelled at a guy one day because he kept talking to me in Arabic like I was supposed to understand him. He kept getting close, waving his arms in the air towards me. I told him to shut the fuck talking to me and that I couldn't understand him. He kept moving and reaching around the truck, making me nervous, so I pointed my rifle at his head. When his hands shot up in the air and he got dead quiet, I knew he got the point.

I couldn't care less about them, for all I know they could be going home and making bombs to use on us, or getting the lay of the land so they could mortar us. Everything that could go wrong crossed my mind; I didn't care either. Better to be on guard all the time than dead.

One day after my shift, Sergeant Brown came knocking on my door.

"Who is it?" I yelled.

"Boney open up," she said in a low voice.

"Yeah, what's up Sarge?"

"First Sergeant wants us in the battalion headquarters."

"O...k. What for?"

"We're getting awards for Najaf. The battalion commander is presenting them after the daily brief."

I was surprised. "What? Ok, hold on."

An award? I couldn't believe it. I threw my gear on and rushed out the door. *Finally,* I thought. *And here I thought no one noticed me.*

We sat quietly in the briefing room next to Saul as the officers ran through the daily brief. Scenarios kept running through my head about what kind of award we would be getting. Something like:

We present this bronze star to Private Boney for his courage and resilience on the front line. Even under pressure he kept his cool and threw himself in the line of fire to provide medical assistance to our troops. Thank you.

When the brief was over, the battalion commander called us up. We stood in front of all the officers in the battalion while he spoke, "It is my honor to present you all with the army commendation medal." We were each handed a green folder with the department of the army seal on the front, our awards attached inside. We stood next to the commander and took pictures as he shook our hands and thanked us for representing the Gamblers with honor.

A soldier read my award out loud:

"To Private First Class Samuel M. Boney for exceptionally meritorious service while attached as a combat medic to the 1st battalion, 5Th Calvary during combat operations in Najaf, Iraq from 5 August 2004 to 28 August 2004. Private first class Boney's technical and tactical knowledge, medical skill, and dedication to duty were instrumental to the successful treatment and evacuation of casualties. His actions reflect great credit upon himself, the Blackjack Brigade, and the United States Army."

Everyone clapped and cheered for us. I looked around smiling, wishing that more than just the officers were there. It would be nice to get recognized in front of our company, to shove this award in everyone's face as proof of what I did. At the same time I realized it didn't matter that much anyway; I didn't want to be recognized by a bunch of fake pricks. It was my job; what I was trained to do. Awards are nice, but knowing I prevailed and saved lives against all odds against me feels a lot better.

Chapter 21: Suicide

In the middle of November we were extended to stay for an extra two months. Our deployment was only supposed to be for a year, so it was no surprise that most of us got pissed off that we weren't going home. Everyone's temper was short after receiving the news.

Scott was mad; his little girl was born a month after we deployed; he only saw her for a week while he was on leave. He kept on talking about how it wasn't fair she was growing up without him. He'd been quiet ever since we got the news; short with anyone who got on his nerves.

Specialist Frey was in a worse situation. Two weeks after we got the news, she received word that her husband had been murdered behind his nightclub along with three of his employees, execution style. She was only allowed to leave for a week to make arrangements for her kids to stay somewhere. She's been chain smoking ever since she got back.

Sergeant Brown took the news the hardest though. One day she came looking for me to drive with her over to South Victory to use the phones. I wanted to call my dad anyway, so I drove with her. If I could do it all over again I would have said no and slammed the door in her face.

She was the first to go in while I sat out in the Humvee. Fifteen minutes later she was stumbling over to me.

"What's up Sergeant? You ok?" Her eyes were halfway closed like she was high on something.

"I need you to come with me," she said, slurring her words. "My husband wants to talk to you."

"Really? I can't leave the vehicle unattended, you know that." I didn't know if she was going crazy or if it was an emergency.

"Don't' worry about it; it's important. He needs to talk to you."

Curious about what was going on, I locked up the vehicle and walked with her back to the phone booth. I picked up the receiver, "Hello?"

"Hey man, dude," he said, sounding hysterical. "You need to get my wife to the hospital now! She just told me she took a bunch of pills to kill herself. You need to get her some help, please!"

I stood silent, looking hard at Brown as she struggled to stand and hold her eyes open. If she wasn't a woman I would have waited until she passed out to say something. I couldn't believe she dragged me into this shit.

"Ok, bye," I said bluntly.

"Thank you, thank you," he said, before I slammed the receiver down.

"Let's fucking go now!" I said furiously.

I held my tongue the best I could, mumbling curse words under my breath until we were out of the trailer. The only thing that made me explode was seeing her stumbling behind me, walking like she was going to pass out. I wasn't about to drag her ass anywhere.

"WHAT THE FUCK IS WRONG WITH YOU, HUH?" I burst out. Everyone around turned and stared at us, but I didn't care; she did this shit on purpose.

"Why did you have to drag me into this, huh? Fuck! Come on move it." I grabbed the back of her vest and pushed her to the ambulance. She was so out of it that I had to help her get in.

"Fucking shit!" I yelled while hitting the steering wheel. "What's wrong with you, huh?" She just sat across from me, silent with her eyes closed, nodding in and out. She tried talking but could only mumble.

For some reason I thought back to Najaf; how she'd been different ever since. Reluctantly, in that moment I could feel her pain. "Shit, hold on, Sarge."

I hauled ass a quarter mile down the road to an aid station and rushed her into the front door.

"I need help! Someone help!" I said as loud as I could. A captain came running around the corner.

"What's wrong soldier?"

"It's my sergeant; she took a bunch pills."

I looked back just in time to see her almost stumble over. The captain and I grabbed her and took her back to a litter.

"I need assistance; we have an overdose!" the captain yelled out. Three medics rushed around the corner and started working on her.

"You can go out in the waiting room," a female soldier told me, walking me out. I called the CP to ask what I should do, and no one answered. A few minutes later the captain approached me.

"Hey soldier. She's refusing to drink the activated charcoal. We're going to have to Medivac her to get her stomach pumped. Do you know how many pills she took?"

"No," I said. "We were at the phone trailer when she told me to talk to her husband. He told me she took a bunch of pills. I rushed her here."

"Ok, well the chopper will be here soon. She asked for you to ride with her. Do you want to?"

"I don't know, let me call my company and ask." Sergeant Robbins answered. I explained the whole situation to him. He told me to ride along because I needed to secure her weapon and they wouldn't have someone get me until the next night. I locked up the vehicle and rode with her on the Blackhawk to the green zone.

She almost didn't make it. They pumped over 40 Valium and 20 Percocet out of her stomach. I wondered how she got so many of them; she must have been planning it for months. I would have never guessed she was serious about it.

"Private Boney, how've things been going for you?" The psychologist looked me in the eye with a slight smile.

"Good I guess," I said. "Just nightmares…every night. I can't sleep. The meds you gave me aren't working anymore."

"Ahh, I see. Can you tell me a little about the dreams? "

"They're always the same; people full of blood, missing limbs, screaming, and explosions. It feels like I'm thrown back in the cemetery every night. Sometimes I can't tell whether I'm dreaming or not."

"MM-hmm," he said, scribbling on his notepad.

"Everything feels so real when I'm asleep; the explosions are hot; I can smell rotting flesh as if it's under my nose. I usually wake up covered in sweat, shivering cold. That last medication you gave me only made my mouth dry; I want to stop dreaming."

"MM-hmm," he said again. "Well I'm going to switch you over to Ambien. It should get you to stay asleep."

"Ok. Do you think it'll help with the dreams?" I asked.

"Hopefully; if not, you can tell me next month and we'll see what we can do, ok?"

"Ok, thanks doc." I stood up, grabbed the prescription and shook his hand.

I knew the meds wouldn't work; it was always the same answer with him, *"Take these and see me next month."* The only help the meds gave me was the slight high I got while on them. I abused them just to feel like I was getting away from it all. It never took away the nightmares; I still woke up drenched in sweat every night.

I tried switching to another company to get back out in the field. It was the only thing that made sense to me since I couldn't stop thinking about it. I went around to different battalions on my days off, to see if they needed a medic. Eventually I was called into the first sergeant's office and had a meeting with him and Sergeant Hall. They told me they would never sign me over to another battalion; I would be going home with them.

I hated them for it. They didn't understand what I wanted. I was just wasting my time escorting shit trucks around and working in the aid-station. Sure, when I first got there I was happy with it; happy with helping any way I could, staying away from the explosions and bullets. That was before I was in combat; it was different now. I felt more useful fighting and saving lives on the front line. Why else was I here?

Chapter 22: Homecoming

It was mid-afternoon when I stepped off the plane onto Ft. Hood. It felt good to be home, at the same time surreal. After 14 months in the dessert, it was weird seeing clean paved roads and new cars driving around. The air was clean and crisp and the temp was nice and cool.

After signing our weapons into the new arms room, we were bused over to the 1st Calvary parade field. Hundreds of people stood cheering and clapping for us. The band played as we marched around the field. A general got on the loudspeaker and welcomed us back before releasing us.

Crowds of people rushed onto the field. Soldiers were crying as their families surrounded them, telling them how much they loved them, clinging on like they'd never seen them before. Scott stood next to his wife, holding his daughter, kissing them both. I looked around for my parents but didn't see them. I had called them ahead of time to let them know when I was coming home.

"Boney?" Hans yelled. He and Jacob both walked up to me.

"Yeah what's up?" I said.

"We should go start celebrating man. Let's go get some booze!" Hans said.

"Sure I'm down. Let's go get our barracks room first."

"Yeah, good point," Jacob said. "We also need someone with a car to get around."

"Maybe someone will give us a ride over at the CP. Come on," I said.

After getting assigned a room in the barracks, I dropped my bags off and went to the CP to call my dad.

"Hello?" he answered.

"What's up old man! Where you at?" I asked.

"At work, where are you?" he said.

"I'm back. We just flew in a couple hours ago. I'm home."

"Awesome! Welcome back home dude. I'm so glad you're back," he said.

"Thanks Dad. I thought you guys were coming to meet me?"

"Yeah I had to work man, I'm sorry. How long before your leave starts.

"Well we have today and tomorrow off. Then we have to work for a week before we have our month leave," I said.

"Ok great. Well, I'm going to come down and pick you up next week when you get off. Then you can spend the week with us, cool?"

It didn't sound good; I wanted to be anywhere but on base. "Ok, yeah that sounds good."

"Cool. What are you doing these first couple days off?" he asked.

"I don't know. A couple of us are going to get together and have a party, have some drinks."

"Alright boy. Well, you take care of yourself; don't drink too much. I'll see you next week. Love you man."

"Love you too Dad," I said before hanging up the phone.

I was surprised to see Sergeant Brown walk through the front door. She smiled at me.

"Sergeant Brown, What the fuck is up?" I said.

"Hey Boney, how are doing?" she said.

"I'm good. How about you?"

"Good, just need to talk to Sergeant Till for a second. You sticking around?"

"Yeah we just got our rooms. I'll be up in 310 when you're done," I said.

"Ok, I'll come knock on your door," she said, walking away.

It felt weird talking to her. I thought for sure she'd be out on a Section 8 by now. She pissed me off with the stunt she pulled, but I was happy she was back and in a better mood. She came knocking on my door half an hour later.

"What's up Sergeant!" Hans belted out behind me.

"Hey Hans, how's it going?" she said.

"Better now that I'm back. You're looking good!"

"Thanks," she said before getting a serious look on her face. "Boney, can I talk to you for a second?"

"Yeah sure, Sarge." I walked out into the `staircase with her, wondering what she could want from me.

"I just wanted to say thank you."

I was shocked. "Thanks for what, Sarge?" I said, acting puzzled.

"Thanks for being there for me. I'm sorry for putting you in that situation. I didn't know what else to do. You saved my life and I just..." She swallowed hard like she was holding back tears. "I just wanted to thank you."

"It's ok Sarge, you don't have to thank me. I'm glad to see you're doing better."

"I am… thanks, Boney. If there's anything I can do for you while I'm still here, let me know; I owe you."

"Alright Sarge, I'll take you up that," I said.

"Ok. What are you planning on doing tonight?" she asked.

"We're looking to get some booze and celebrate."

"You guys want to have a party at my house? My husband wants to meet you."

I thought it would be weird, but we didn't have a car to get around and I definitely didn't want to stay here.

"Fuck yeah Sarge!" I shouted. "Let me get dressed. I'll tell everyone else. Yeah!"

She drove us all over to the class six on base to get liquor. The place was packed full of troops. We waited over a half an hour in line to check out. We didn't make it off base before we cracked into our bottles. We were lit by the time we walked through her front door. Her husband was waiting for us, blasting music, already getting drunk himself.

"Welcome home guys!" he said, raising a beer in his hand. We all cheered as he ran over and shook our hands while Brown introduced us.

"And this is Boney," she said, pointing at me.

"The Boney? Man I'm so glad to finally meet you. My wife has told me so much about you." He reached out his hand and I shook it.

"Nice to meet you too man," I said.

"Dude thank you so much for getting my wife help," he said, still gripping my hand. "You know you saved her life."

"Ah man it was nothing, thanks. I wish it didn't have to happen."

"Me neither. But I really mean it." He looked at me hard, "Thank you. She told me what you did over in the sandbox fighting in Najaf. You're a hero man, I hope you know that."

"Thanks, I appreciate it. I was just doing my job."

"See I wish I had more guys like you in my company. You're a real warrior, Hooah!" he shouted.

"Hooah!" I shouted loud; so did everyone else.

We played drinking games and listened to music most of the night. Sergeant Brown stumbled over to me halfway through the night, "Boney, Boney. You gotta check this out. I fucked shit up the other day," she said, heavily slurring her words. "Our friends have a ranch where we go shooting every weekend; check it out!"

She played a video of her holding an automatic rifle shooting at trees and cans. She fired shot after shot while walking up to the targets. When she ran out of ammo she dropped the rifle, took out a pistol started firing at a tree stump a foot or two away.

"Fucking sweet huh?" she asked.

"Yeah that's nice," I said, not the least bit interested.

Where was this person when we were getting attacked? I thought, remembering how she had cowered behind her rifle, not firing a single shot. "You should come with us next time we go. I know you can shoot good," she said.

"Yeah sure, I'll come. Just let me know when you go," I said, still watching the video. She dropped the pistol and pulled out a knife and started stabbing the tree, screaming. Her husband walked up behind us and started cheering her on, "Yeah baby get'em, get'em. Wooho!"

She showed me four videos of her doing the same thing with her husband. After seeing her try to kill herself I wouldn't think that it would be safe for her to have a gun, let alone shoot one. I made it a point not to go shooting with her. I didn't want to be on the other side of her rifle when she pulls crazy out.

*   *   *

My heart throbbed in my throat as I watched B kick in the door. I toss a grenade in and step back with my rifle ready. The explosion pulsed through my body. I rushed through the door, spraying the room with my rifle. My chest burned as the smell of rotting flesh filled the room. Everything went dark; Screams echoed all around me, "I'm hit! Medic! Help!"

Another huge explosion rocked me; everything shook. My body felt like it was going to shake apart. I saw blood, bright red blood all over the ground. I struggled to breathe; the rotting smell got overwhelming.

My heart leaped as a man in grey rags ran in front of me. I pulled the trigger over and over again, feeling my weapon kick into my shoulder. A flash of light engulfed me with every blast as rage took over. Someone screamed for a medic again. The next thing I know I'm staring at a bloody hole; my hands were soaked in blood as I held his head, watching it ooze out.

A voice in another language woke me. It sounded like they were praying over a loud speaker. I opened my eyes slowly still feeling drowsy. All of a sudden there was a loud bang. Thinking it was a mortar I jumped up and reached for my weapon to run outside… but it wasn't there. *What the fuck?* I looked around the room not knowing where I was. I got on the ground and looked for my weapon under the bed.

"Where's my weapon?" I said, my heart beating faster as I tried to think. "Who took my weapon?!" I started freaking out. I looked at my wrist to see what time it was, but there was just an outline of a watch on my tanned skin.

Suddenly, a rush of information started coming back to me. The last couple months: getting back stateside, signing my weapon over, and going on leave. I sat down with my head in my hands to try calming myself down. *You're home; you're home.* It felt like I was dreaming. What happened, why am I back here?

After getting dressed I walked over to the DEFAC with last night's dream still fresh in my mind. It felt like I was just in combat yesterday. Being on base in civilians didn't feel right. I ate breakfast halfway in a daze, feeling like I was going to wake up in my trailer any minute, but I never did.

After I ate, I jumped into my truck and drove over to the class six and bought a bottle of patron; I took a couple swigs in the parking lot before driving off again. A thought crossed my mind; *I wasn't really here, that this wasn't real.* I turned the music up loud and sang along to drown out my thoughts. It felt weird though. Usually music made me happy, but I couldn't feel anything at all. *This had to be a dream,* I thought. No one else was on the road with me. *I should just kill myself, run my truck off the road. Maybe I'll wake up then, I'll feel like myself again.* I pressed the gas down hard, screeching my wheels on the pavement as my truck lurched forward. I gained speed fast. Once the speedometer reached seventy miles per hour, I let go of the wheel.

I watched as my truck started veering off the road, headed towards a brick wall with a cement barricade on the side of the street. My heart started beating harder and harder. The world spun around me as it got harder to breathe. My eyes teared up, clouding my view of the road, so I closed them and got ready to wake up.

No! A voice screamed in my head. *Don't do it, stop!* My chest suddenly burned with pain. I didn't want to die, but I don't want to feel like I'm not alive. *Stop!* The voice shouted. I opened my eyes and pressed the brakes as my truck jumped the curb. I jerked the wheel and swerved it back onto the road and stopped.

Tears started pouring out as I came to the realization that this was all real. I screamed and punching the wheel, *why wasn't I happy? Why did I feel this way?*

A car honked at me from behind as I sat there. I drove a block and parked in an empty lot and started chain smoking. I needed help but didn't want anyone to know. The last thing I needed was to be treated like I was crazy; I didn't want to get kicked out of the Army. I just needed to talk to someone; someone who understands what's going on with me.

I took out my phone and called Sergeant Hill.

"Hello?" she answered.

"Sergeant, It's me, Boney."

"What's up Boney? Something wrong?"

"Yes Sergeant, I'm...I don't know," I said.

"Boney, talk to me. What's going on?"

"I'm not feeling right, Sarge. I think something's wrong with me," I said, panicked,

"Ok Boney, calm down and breathe; I'm gonna get you through this."

*   *   *

After talking to a therapist, they diagnosed me as being bi-polar. They said I'd been having spurts

271

of manic-depression and that's what had been sending me into the waves of feelings and dreams that I couldn't control.

When I started meds, my mood became stable and I became able to focus on reality. The only thing is that the meds never took away the dead feeling in my body – the numbness, rage, and anger I had rooted deep down.

Chapter 23: Selection

After being home for seven months, a stop loss stop leave was put in effect for our brigade; we were headed back to Iraq in less than a year. It surprised me that we would be going back so soon. I wanted to go, just not with this battalion. I'd rather be in an infantry or artillery squad, going out on missions, not stuck in an aid-station or escorting around shit trucks, waiting to get hit by a mortar.

After finding out I couldn't get transferred to a different battalion, I figured trying out for Special Forces wasn't a bad idea. It had always interested me because I would automatically become a sergeant and wear a Green Beret. I went over to the recruiting office on base to ask about being medical sergeant.

The recruiter told me a couple things to do in order to get approval for selection. One was to get my doctor to sign off that I would be fine without meds. The next thing was to get it approved by my first sergeant and commander.

It was hard getting my doctors to sign off. They wouldn't approve me unless I could go three months without having an episode. I knew I'd be fine; it would give me time to train so I would be in top shape. I could stay in control as long as my mind was actively doing something.

My first sergeant said I wasn't what they were looking for; he wanted me to think hard about what I was doing. Not everyone makes it through, and not many survive in combat. But after explaining the fight in Najaf and the fact that I wanted to be a part of something bigger, he approved me.

I trained three times a day; PT in the morning, weights in the afternoon, and running three miles at night. A few days out of the week, my friend dropped me off with my fifty-five-pound rucksack ten miles from base. I marched back along trails without a radio or a phone, sometimes running as fast as I could, each time getting quicker.

I was eventually cleared by my doctors and scheduled to ship out to Fort Bragg for selection in the middle of November. I felt stronger than ever. Staying fit and motivated helped me make it through that far. Nightmares still haunted me, but I was too focused on where I wanted to go to be bothered. When I was restless at night I would get up and run until I crashed.

*   *   *

Keep going. Don't stop. Keep moving. I'm beat down and tired, marching on a dirt trail through the woods at Fort Bragg. There are just a few soldiers around me. People get weeded out the more miles we go. It feels like I've been walking for days, months even. My shins burn and my feet are numb. It's taking everything in me to put one foot in front of the other and move on.

People say that hell week is the worst; I never imagined it to be this brutal. The instructors were trying their best to break us mentally and physically; it was working too. We started out with over three hundred troops two weeks ago; eighty to ninety have dropped out.

We were put through the wringer on the first day of selection. We woke up early and did rifle PT, doing hand raises, push-ups, sit-ups, and jumping jacks with dummy rifles in our hands; they smoked us for two hours straight.

275

We did log training immediately after. We stood in seven-person lines and did squats and lifts with phone poles for another two hours. I reached muscle failure halfway through log PT. I'm sure most of the guys in my group did, seeing as the pole got harder and harder to lift as time went on. The instructors walked back and forth in between us, watching closely. They didn't yell like drill sergeants, they just watched and sometimes wrote notes. By the end of the day, twenty soldiers dropped out. I stood in formation and watched as six guys from my team walked over and stood in front of the instructors' building. I thought they were pathetic for dropping out just because of a little PT.

On the second day we were awakened after two hours of sleep and told to get in formation for a road march in the middle of the night; it was cold and misty out. After getting in formation we were told to empty out our rucksacks and drop our pants for inspection. They told us from the jump we weren't supposed to wear or bring anything other than what we were told.

We stood shivering with our hands raised, waiting for the sergeants to check us off. A couple people had long johns on and were written up for it.

After twenty minutes I was checked off, packed up and standing ready for the road march. Ten people stood outside the instructors' building before they blew the whistle for us to start.

I marched through the woods right behind a group of guys. We were all in the lead; running down a beaten path through the woods. The instructors told us they put glow sticks out at turns. Thirty minutes into it we started passing houses and mailboxes. A couple guys said we might have missed a turn but none of us saw a glow stick so we kept moving on. A truck drove past us, flashing the headlights. A sergeant stopped and got out asking us why we were so far off track. He told us we missed the turn a mile back.

We all turned around and hauled ass back down the road. We ended up being the last group to finish. An instructor came over to tell us to pay better attention next time, but I knew that glow stick wasn't there the first time we passed it, how could I miss a bright green light in the dark. My legs were killing me by the time I made it to my bunk.

It was non-stop since then; I swear my body was going to fall apart. My feet felt broken. The most sleep I got in one day was two hours. I had to keep telling myself not to quit as I passed by soldiers sitting on their rucksacks, waiting for an instructor to pick them up to drop out. *I'm not like them,* I thought. *I'm not a quitter. Keep moving.*

I made it into a clearing and looked around. Two people were far ahead of me, no one behind. Not having someone around to talk to left me with just my thoughts. I thought a lot about the things I've gone through in life; the experiences that pushed me into the place I was in now. My mind kept jumping to combat, the people I helped save, the ones I killed.

I started feeling weird; like a bunch of acid from my stomach was built up in the back of my throat. I started seeing vivid colors; it felt like I was in some sort of dream. The weight of my pack got heavier and my right knee started throbbing.

I heard a voice, "2'oclock!" I stopped and raised my weapon. *What the fuck was that?* I shook my head trying to regain my senses. I looked at my rifle and made a note that it wasn't real; that voice wasn't real either. I moved at a faster pace, trying to catch up to the guys who were in front of me.

Do you really want this? I asked myself. Of course I do, why else was I here? Making it into Special Forces is a goal of mine. The only thing I wanted was to make it on an A-Team, to be the best soldier I could be; in the fight, part of something more than just an assistant role.

My mind started getting cloudy. I saw myself sitting in a chair laughing with people around me. There were kids playing on my lap and a woman smiling, but I couldn't recognize their faces. I got a heavy, warm feeling in my chest.

I shook my head, trying snap out of whatever was happening. *What's going on?* I never thought about having a family before, so where did that come from. I kept marching, thinking of what life would be like if I had one. Sure it would be nice, but it didn't fit in with what I wanted. The only thing I wanted was to fight for my country and save lives. I never thought of anything else except that... and death.

I crossed the finish line back at camp and sat down in formation to wait for the other guys to finish. So many things were running through my mind, making me question what I was doing with my life. My head got heavy and started pounding, making me dizzy. I slammed half my water bottle and took deep breaths to calm myself down.

As I was looking around at everyone I heard gunfire in the distance. I thought it was a group starting their night ops training because it was getting dark out. Out the corner of my eye I saw someone fall off the top of a building and land on the ground. My heart sank for a split second in shock. Then I was filled with a burst of energy, jumping up quickly to run over and help. I stopped short, realizing no one was there.

"You alright man?" a soldier asked me.

"I don't know," I said, pointing over to the building. "Did you see that?"

"See what?" he said.

"I swear I just saw someone fall off that building."

"Um, I don't think so man. Maybe you should talk to someone; you don't sound good."

I must be losing my mind, I thought. "No, I'm fine man." I walked back to my gear.

"You sure?" he asked.

"Yeah I'm good." I didn't know what to believe; it felt like I was trapped in between reality and a dream. My heart raced, sweat poured off my face. For some reason I couldn't calm down; I felt like hitting someone, killing something.

When the rest of the soldiers crossed the finish line we were released for dinner. On the way over to the DEFAC I saw a parachute light shoot up into the sky and hang in mid-air, saturating everything in light. My mind shot back to the cemetery. I started hearing gunfire zip past me. When I looked around it looked like I was in the cemetery.

A person dressed in rags ran from behind a grave so I pointed my rifle toward him and tried pulling the trigger. When it didn't fire I realized it was a dummy. I lost it.

"FUCK! What the fuck is going on?" I said, turning in circles, trying to figure out where I was.

"Dude, calm down," I heard someone yell at me. "What's going on?"

"I don't know! I FUCKING DON'T KNOW!"

Chapter 24: 86'd

I was medically discharged from the Army in 2006; twenty-three years old; left to deal with my problems alone. What I wanted to do with my life wasn't clear. I remember asking my Dad if I could stay with him for a while, but he wasn't having it. He told me he never had the option to live at home when he was an adult, so why should I? I explained to him what I was going through, but I don't think he fully understood. That left me alone, trying to figure out what to do with my life. It was hard going every day without a sense of direction. I had depended on the army for that for the past three years.

I didn't have a job or a place to stay so I ended up crashing at a friend's house for a few months while they were away for training. During that time I got hooked on ecstasy. I rolled all day every day, trying to kill the emptiness and anger inside; it gave me a false sense of happiness. I stayed high without sleeping for days at a time, only to pass out for a couple hours and do it all again. One day I fell asleep and someone I had invited to the house took off with my friend's stereo. After that happened, I stopped taking pills and started looking for something to do with my life.

My plan had been to get a job in the medical field when I got out, but now I didn't want to be reminded of anything that happened in war. The only thing I could imagine doing with my life was cooking, something far away from the medical field. So I enrolled in Le Cordon Bleu in Minnesota to become a chef.

There was something about the order and discipline in the kitchen that made me love it. It was like following orders in the military; one mistake and everything could go wrong. I ended up working for restaurants all over town, learning new techniques for cooking. For my internship I worked on a cruise line in Hawaii. It was a good thing for me because it didn't allow me to think about anything else but cooking, and I could work out anytime of the day. I worked two jobs, 12-16 hours a day. I tried my hardest to always be on the go so I wouldn't have to sit and think, so I drank heavily on my time off.

I met a woman named Jessica while I was bar hopping downtown Minneapolis. She knocked on a window while I was walking by and waved at me. I thought she was the most beautiful woman I've ever seen. After a few months of dating she got pregnant. It was a wake-up call for me to clean up my act and start thinking about my baby's future, so we moved in together to try and start a family. That's when my demons started catching up with me.

I started drinking a 5th of vodka every three days, on my own trying to drown out flashbacks and nightmares. It helped me cope with the numbness I felt inside. I never talked to anyone about it because I knew they wouldn't understand. Who could understand?

My body felt like it was falling apart too. What used to be an ache in service turned into chronic pain. It started with my back; I couldn't go a minute in the day without feeling like there was a hot knife stuck in my spine, burning my muscles. I started having migraines four days out of the week, making it impossible to work most days. Then my knees started hurting every time I ran, forcing me to stop. I was pissed because that was the only way I could get my aggression out. Running had become a release for me and now it was gone.

I went to the VA to find out what was going on; took me months to be seen. The only thing my doctors could tell after multiple tests was that I was born with a slight curve in my spine. Along with wearing heavy gear and fighting in Iraq they say I virtually had no cushion in between my disks; my spine had started deteriorating in multiple places. They also said my knees were shot due to the same factors. I was diagnosed with severe osteoarthritis in both my knees. Only twenty-seven years old and I would never be able to run again or have a job that needed me to move around.

They put me on multiple narcotics to help with the pain. None of them helped me; I just got hooked. I fell back into my old habits quickly; taking more drugs than I should to try to kill the pain, the nightmares, and the demons that lived inside me. Darkness grew inside and there was nothing I could do to stop it.

I didn't know how deep it ran until the day my daughter was born. I couldn't feel anything when I first saw her; my emotions were numb and distant.

Before she was born I imagined tearing up or feeling immense warmth in my heart when I set eyes on her; instead, I felt nothing. And it wasn't only her; I started feeling the same way with Jessica. It made me angry that I couldn't feel anything; it felt like not being alive, most of the time.

The only emotions I felt most days were anger and hate. I would wake up tired and frustrated when I had had nightmares the night before. I would go through the day having flashbacks; lashing out at Jessica when I felt too overwhelmed. We fought so much it got to the point where I would scream at her like she was a soldier in the military just so she wouldn't fight back. I didn't care about making her cry; people who cried were weak, nothing gets accomplished by crying.

One day I met a veteran while going through therapy at the VA hospital. We ended up sharing some stories. Once I started shaking after telling a story. He said I might have Post Traumatic Stress Disorder, PTSD for short. For some reason my doctors never brought that up. He said that smoking marijuana would help some of my problems. I had just smoked it every now and then for fun; I had never tried it to help with my symptoms before.

I started smoking every day and noticed that I was sleeping better at night. For some reason it stopped my nightmares completely, allowing me to get a full night's rest. It also helped me with my emotions. I felt happier for a change. It kept my mind off the pain so I was able to function more throughout the day. It helped so much I even stopped taking the pain pills. It's been a miracle to me that it worked so well.

Smoking and drinking didn't sit well with Jessica and we ended up fighting more than ever. She didn't see using as being helpful. It got to the point where I moved out one day because I was tired of explaining myself to anyone. I went through war for my country and survived; if marijuana helps me stay in control, then I'm going to use it.

I moved into an apartment by myself, thinking it would take away my problems, but it just made them worse. I didn't feel safe anywhere. I would hear things like noises that sounded like guns and explosions. It made me freak out to the point where I was locking myself in the house. I didn't go anywhere unless it was to work or unless someone was with me.

The shit that was going through my mind every day was scary. I couldn't control it. I was never outside alone without thinking something bad was going to happen; not having a weapon made me feel powerless. I thought people wanted to kill me. I was constantly watching my surroundings, staring at people, thinking of how I would kill them if they tried anything. I even wore a knife on me just in case.

I was lost; so far gone. The only thing I could think of was dying. Every day I thought of killing myself, not wanting to be tormented anymore.

*   *   *

I can't do this. What's the fucking point? Am I even alive? No one thinks about me; no one cares. I don't want to be here. Tears ran down my face as I sat on the ground. *If I were dead I wouldn't have pain; I wouldn't have to suffer.*

"Ahhh!" I screamed out. It echoed around the apartment. I remembered the knife I had dropped on the ground; *Fuck it!* I ran over and picked it up, grasping it tight in my hand, staring at my wrist.

The veins popping out showed me the perfect spot I could cut.

I got on my knees, closed my eyes and rocked back and forth. *Do it.* My mind was made up; this was it. *Do it!* I couldn't help but to think of how much it would hurt. *DO IT!* I brought the knife closer and cried.

My phone started ringing. I froze in place and listened as it kept ringing, hoping it would stop. "Fuck!" I threw the knife down and walked over to the phone to see who it was. I picked up when I saw it was Jessica.

"What?" I answered rudely.

"Hold on," she said. Then I heard the phone rustle a bit.

"Daddy?" a little voice rang in my ear. It felt like everything in the world came to a standstill as she started talking. "Daddy?"

"Hey Butternut, how's my girl?" I tried talking normal, but my voice was raspy as tears rolled down my face.

"Good," she said. "Guess what?"

"What is it babes?"

"I made you something at school," she said excitedly.

"You did? What is it?"

"I can't tell you. Where are you?" She sounded so innocent, totally clueless to the world I was living in.

"Oh I'm at my apartment, I just got off work."

"Oh. Are you coming over? I want to see you."

At that second my heart felt like it shattered. *What was I about to do?* Tears poured down my face as I became ashamed of trying to ruin her world.

"Hello? Daddy?" she asked, thinking I hung up.

"I'm here babe."

"Are you coming over?"

"Yeah babe, I'll come over. I've got a couple things to do tonight, but I'll come over tomorrow. Is that ok?"

"Ok, yeah dat's good." She sounded excited. I could hear her whisper to her mom, "He's coming over tomorrow."

"Ok Daddy. I love you."

"I love you too baby girl. You get a good night's rest, ok?" I pretended to kiss her; she did the same back.

"Ok, bye Daddy."

"Bye Princess."

When she hung up, I put my phone down. I curled up in a ball on the floor and I cried, hard. I regretted trying to kill myself. How could I be so stupid? My daughter needed me; she loves me. She didn't know about my past; she didn't care about anything else but loving me, no matter what.

I had forgotten about it – the vision in selection – how I was laughing with kids in my lap, sitting next to my wife, surrounded with love and happiness. I wanted that. For some reason it felt like I could have it, but how? How could I change the person I'd become? I was filled with anger, frustration, and emptiness; I couldn't love anyone....

Then I remembered something I had experienced – the thing that had calmed me when I was being mortared in the cemetery. The warm bright orange light; how it wrapped me up with love and comfort even in the midst of terror.

My grandma was there, praying right next to me. I wondered if her prayer changed the outcome of what happened. It should have ended a lot different. A mortar should have killed us, the building should have collapsed, I should have been shot. There were way too many close calls for it to just be a coincidence.

One thing my grandma told me, *"whenever it feels like the world is against you and you need help, pray. The Lord is always by your side."*

So, I put my hands together and prayed. I asked God how I could get through this. I asked him to give me strength to get better and to take away all the bad thoughts so I could be with my daughter. I asked how I could make things better with Jessica. What did I need to do to get better?

After I prayed I had a feeling that I needed to talk to Jessica. I needed to start telling people how I really felt inside instead of always running. How was I supposed to get better if all I did was hold everything in and deal with it myself? I was still fighting a war inside; my experience with war was that you can't fight it on your own and expect to win.

I picked up my phone and started dialing a number off a magnet on my fridge. A woman answered.

"Veterans crisis hotline. This is Sarah."

Tears kept pouring down my face. "Sarah, I need help. I'm going to kill myself if I don't get help!"

Author's Note

War is painful. It's an untamed beast that savagely destroys thousands of lives every year. A demon that possesses the minds of wounded soldiers that survive its grasp; to torment them day and night about the hell they survived, leaving them void, lifeless at times. It destroys families, leaving children without fathers and mothers, sisters and brothers, sons and daughters. It's relentless as hell and it'll plague the world forever.

Death and chaos followed me everywhere I went; I never felt safe, not even within the safety of a base. Being a combat medic means to sacrifice yourself for the safety of other people, even if it means dying or losing a part of yourself in the process. There are three unwritten rules that all combat medics follow. The first, good men will die. The second, Doc can't save everyone. The third, Doc will go through hell to break rules one and two. The hell that I went through changed me. War changes everyone, whether they admit to it or not.

PTSD

Post-Traumatic Stress Disorder develops in some people that have seen or lived through a scary or dangerous event. It causes people to isolate themselves from things that remind them of the experience. It makes a person feel numb and void, forcing them to be less interested in things they used to enjoy. It causes people to hear and see things that aren't around in the form of a flashback making it feel as real as the first time. Recurring nightmares won't allow a person to forget what happened. It's a tough fight to go through on your own.

If you know someone who's currently struggling with PTSD, be there. Even if they push you away because they think you won't understand, be there with open arms to catch them when they fall, even if you don't understand, because no one else will. Well over 22 veterans commit suicide each day in America, proof that war never ends; even after you're safe at home. I almost became a statistic, but by the grace of God I was given the strength to fight and go after a better life.

In time I've found that talking to counselors has helped with sorting through the pain and darkness I'm feeling. It also helped that I had a loving girlfriend who was willing to listen and try to make things work as best as possible. If I didn't have her I wouldn't be here today.

If you're a veteran and need help, go talk to someone. If you can be seen at the Veterans Hospital, talk to a counselor. Find out if they can get you help. If that doesn't work, try talking to family or friends, anyone you can to get whatever you have trapped inside, out. Find God as well. Try to build a strong relationship with Him because with His help you can make it through the impossible.

If you are in need to talk to someone because you're in a crisis, do what I did and call the Veterans Crisis line: 1-800-273-8255.

EPILOGUE

Building a relationship with God has helped me understand some of the things that I went through. It's not possible to go through life without having storms. There's an evil in this world that tries to do everything it can to bring us down; to make us think we're less than what God created us to be. But there's something greater inside of us than anything in this world.

People weren't born to lose; we were born to win – win at any cost at whatever obstacle comes our way; it's how God made us. But it's hard to feel like a winner when the whole world was made to be against you; that's how it feels to be a soldier back home from war.

Until you've been in combat, fighting day and night through blood, sweat, and tears, trying to win a battle that seems unwinnable and live to tell about it, you will never know the real struggle a soldier has to go through.

After years of therapy I still struggle with nightmares, flashbacks, and feeling normal. I know I may never feel normal. The difference now is that

I have a support system whenever times get rough. God helped me understand that life was more than what had happened in my past; he brought me the love of family to help guide me through.

My mind used to be focused solely on war and using drugs to help me cope. I didn't think I had time to live to worry about anything else but death. Now my focus is on love, family, and salvation; the only important things in life.

CPSIA information can be obtained
at www.ICGtesting.com
Printed in the USA
LVHW050536281222
736016LV00001B/144

9 781533 330277